Praise for *On the Ground in Afghanistan: Counterinsurgency in Practice*

"Great format and important lessons learned. . . . This book should be mandatory reading for all Marines."

—General Richard D. Hearney, USMC (Ret), former Assistant Commandant of the Marine Corps

"A superb book, chock-full of multinational combat examples with great maps and photographs. This well-written book should be mandatory reading for special operators and unit commanders. *On the Ground in Afghanistan* blends theory and practice in an effort to adapt to war in unique and often peculiar contexts."

—Joseph J. Collins, professor of national security strategy at the National War College and former deputy assistant secretary of defense for stability operations

"Effective counterinsurgency is about learning and adapting to local conditions. This volume lets the small unit leader profit from 15 different fights—and should convince him or her that there is no one best way to fight an insurgent."

—T. X. Hammes, author of *The Sling and the Stone: On War in the 21st Century*

"A completely outstanding piece of work."

—David Kilcullen, author of *The Accidental Guerrilla* and *Counterinsurgency*

"This is a book that will be of great interest to soldiers, policy makers, and scholars alike—it is an invaluable addition to the literature on insurgency in general and the Afghan conflict in particular."

—Bruce Hoffman, author of *Inside Terrorism* and director of the Center for Peace and Security Studies, Georgetown University

ON THE GROUND IN
AFGHANISTAN
COUNTERINSURGENCY IN PRACTICE

JERRY MEYERLE I MEGAN KATT I JIM GAVRILIS

A joint publication of CNA and Marine Corps University Press

This book represents the best opinion of CNA at the time of printing. The views expressed in it do not necessarily represent the opinions of the U.S. Department of the Navy or the U.S. Marine Corps.

CNA Corporation
4825 Mark Center Drive
Alexandria, Virginia 22311
www.cna.org

Marine Corps University Press
3078 Upshur Avenue
Quantico, Virginia 22134
www.tecom.usmc.mil/mcu/mcupress

For sale by the Superintendent of Documents, U.S. Government Printing Office
Internet: bookstore.gpo.gov Phone: toll free (866) 512-1800; DC area (202) 512-1800
Fax: (202) 512-2104 Mail: Stop IDCC, Washington, DC 20402-0001

ISBN 978-0-16-090258-1

Dedication

U.S. Marines talk with leaders at a meeting in the Nawa District, Helmand Province. (Photo by Cpl Artur Shvartsberg, U.S. Marine Corps)

The authors wish to dedicate this book to the many U.S. and NATO service members who have risked life and limb to help stabilize Afghanistan—among them Sergeant William Cahir, U.S. Marine Corps, who appears in this photo (*sitting, center left*). Sergeant Cahir was killed while on patrol in southern Afghanistan on 13 August 2009.

Contents

British Army and Marines

Dutch Army and Marines

Canadian Army

Conclusion   165

Notes   177

About the Authors   186

Maps and Figures

Acronyms and Abbreviations

ABP	Afghan Border Police	IED	improvised explosive device
ADT	agribusiness development team	IO	information operations
AMF	Afghan Militia Forces	ISAF	International Security Assistance Force
ANA	Afghan National Army	ISI	Pakistan's Interservices Intelligence
ANCOP	Afghan National Civil Order Police	JPCC	Joint Provincial Coordination Center
ANP	Afghan National Police	JSOA	joint special operations area
ANSF	Afghan National Security Forces	MEDCAP	medical civic assistance program
AO	area of operations	MSST	military stabilization support team
CAG	civil affairs group	NATO	North Atlantic Treaty Organization
CERP	commander's emergency response program	NCO	noncommissioned officer
CNAT	counternarcotics advisory team	NGO	nongovernmental organization
COIN	counterinsurgency	ODA	operational detachment alpha
COP	combat outpost	OMLT	operational mentor and liaison team
CP	checkpoint	PB	patrol base
FB	firebase	PRT	provincial reconstruction team
FDD	focused district development	PSYOP	psychological operations
FLET	forward lines of enemy troops	RIAB	radio in a box
FOB	forward operating base	RPG	rocket-propelled grenade
FPF	force protection facility	SF	U.S. Army Special Forces
HA	hectare	TF	task force
HiG	Hizbul-e-Islami Gulbuddin	UN	United Nations
HVT	high-value target	UNODC	United Nations Office on Drugs and Crime

Preface and Acknowledgments

This book provides a glimpse into what relatively small military units—teams, platoons, companies, and highly dispersed battalions—have done to roll back the insurgency in some of the more remote areas of Afghanistan. The focus is on counterinsurgency at the tactical and local levels.

The book includes 15 vignettes about different units from the U.S. Marines, U.S. Army, and U.S. Army Special Forces; the British army and marines; the Dutch army and marines; and the Canadian army. The case studies cover 10 provinces in the south and east of Afghanistan. They describe the diverse conditions the units faced in these provinces, how they responded to these conditions, what worked and what did not, and the successes involved in these operations.

This study would not have been possible without the generous help of Marines and soldiers from the U.S., British, Dutch, and Canadian militaries. They spent many hours with the authors going over the details of past events and relating their experiences.

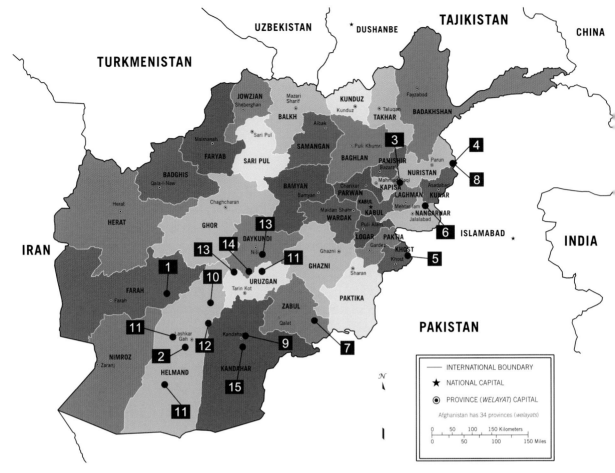

Vignette Locations

1. U.S. Marine Platoon, Gulistan, Farah, 2008

2. U.S. Marine Battalion, Nawa, Helmand, 2009

3. U.S. Marine Advisors, Tagab Valley, Kapisa, 2008

4. U.S. Army Battalion, Kunar and Nuristan, 2007–2008

5. U.S. Army Battalion, Khost, 2004–2008

6. U.S. Army Battalion, Nangarhar, 2005–2009

7. U.S. Army Special Forces Team, Kandahar and Zabul, 2003–2005

8. Three U.S. Army Special Forces Teams, Kunar and Nuristan, 2004–2005

9. U.S. Army Special Forces Team, Kandahar, 2003–2004

10. UK-Led Task Force, Musa Qala, Helmand, 2006–2009

11. British Marine Battalion, Uruzgan and Helmand, 2008–2009

12. British Army Advisors, Sangin, Helmand, 2009

13. Two Dutch Army Companies, Uruzgan, 2006–2009

14. Dutch Marine Company, Deh Rashaan, Uruzgan, 2009

15. Canadian Soldiers and Engineers, Dand, Kandahar, 2009

Introduction

Only in the fall of 2009 did counterinsurgency became the centerpiece of U.S. strategy in Afghanistan, yet Coalition troops had been fighting an insurgency there since at least 2003, before the outbreak of violence in Iraq and the development of the new counterinsurgency field manual. Soldiers and Marines in Afghanistan made many mistakes; they also employed many sound practices learned through hard experience. This book captures some of those practices and the unique conditions under which they were developed.

Military units that deployed to remote areas of Afghanistan learned to operate in an unfamiliar environment: a desperately poor, war-torn agricultural society with no functioning central government or modern economy, its population dispersed across thousands of tiny villages cut off from one another by unforgiving terrain with virtually no infrastructure. Coalition troops found themselves fighting a politically astute rural insurgency tied closely to the population. The political problems driving the violence were exceedingly opaque, complex, and localized.

Small units[*] operating in extremely remote regions of Afghanistan, often completely isolated from their higher headquarters, had to navigate the treacherous waters of internecine tribal politics. They had to identify potential supporters and detractors while retaining some semblance of neutrality; empower local leaders without being manipulated by deceitful power brokers and corrupt officials; and fight off large numbers of proficient enemy fighters without harming civilians or making enemies of powerful tribes, some of whose members were involved in attacks on Coalition troops—all in an environment of persistent insurgent intimidation.

---

[*] The term "small unit" is used in different ways. Publications about small unit infantry tactics often use the term to refer to units smaller than a platoon. The U.S. Marine Corps' *Small Unit Leaders' Guide to Counterinsurgency* uses the term to refer to formations at the company level and below. For the purposes of this study, battalion-sized formations are also considered small units, since the battalions covered in this book were spread out over very large areas, with companies and platoons scattered about on small bases. The vignettes in this book focus on the actions of these companies and platoons under the strategic direction of their battalion commanders.

Despite these challenges, many small units on the ground met with successes rarely captured in the media. Many of these lessons have yet to make their way up the chain of command or be reflected at the strategic level.

The purpose of this book is to shed light on what small military units did in different parts of Afghanistan from the earliest years of the insurgency in 2003 to the surge of U.S. forces in 2009. It is, in part, a collection of their experiences. It describes the varying conditions faced by small units in remote areas, how they responded to these conditions, what worked, and what did not.

This is not a book about policy, strategy, or national politics in Afghanistan, nor is it a book about counterinsurgency theory. Many others have written on these topics. The focus of this book is on small-unit counterinsurgency tactics and local-level politics.

There is a tremendous gap in understanding this aspect of the war. It is at the small-unit level that counterinsurgency is actually practiced and that evidence for the success or failure of the overall U.S. effort in Afghanistan is to be found.

This book includes 15 vignettes of counterinsurgency operations by military units, many of them deployed to some of the most remote and difficult areas of Afghanistan. These vignettes describe in detail the conditions faced by small units at the tactical level and their responses to local conditions. The insights in this book are based entirely on the information contained in these vignettes and on the views of officers involved in the operations described. The research is based almost entirely on interviews with these officers.

The vignettes are written like storyboards: each is followed by a brief conclusion covering the main themes and lessons learned. The authors chose this approach because it is an effective method of describing and analyzing individual operations by small units in remote areas.

The vignettes cover 10 provinces in the south and east of Afghanistan from 2003 through 2009. There are examples of operations by the U.S. Marines, U.S. Army, and U.S. Army Special Forces; British soldiers and marines; Dutch soldiers and marines; and the Canadian army. The book describes operations by battalions, companies, platoons, special forces teams, and small groups of trainers embedded with the Afghan army and police.

A Different Sort of Conflict

As the war in Iraq winds down, the one in Afghanistan is reaching new heights. Soldiers and Marines are heading to Afghanistan in large numbers to retake the initiative and implement a far-reaching counterinsurgency strategy. Many learned counterinsurgency in the cities of Iraq and are now employing its principles in the villages of Afghanistan. The basic principles remain valid: a focus on the population, the primacy of politics, restraint in the use of force, and good governance.

Afghanistan, however, is a different sort of place. It is an underdeveloped society with an extremely dispersed, almost entirely rural population. The insurgents are based in villages and have little support in the cities. Many Afghans have never left their villages and possess little knowledge of the outside world—to many, the Kabul government is like a foreign entity. In order to influence a population that is so spread out, troops must disperse across vast distances and operate from isolated bases. They must deal with conservative rural communities, most of them illiterate, for whom national identity and public service are unfamiliar concepts. Islam, tradition, and ties of blood are far more important.

Afghanistan's population is extremely fragmented. The politics of each village, town, and valley are a hornet's nest of small tribes and clans fighting constantly over land, water, and other resources. These conflicts have little connection to larger political dynamics, or even to those of adjacent areas. The Pashtun tribes of Afghanistan, who make up the bulk of the insurgency, have long been a fractured and quarrelsome lot, fiercely protective of their autonomy, suspicious of outsiders, and distrustful of nearly all forms of authority.

Decades of insurgency and civil war have destroyed much of the traditional leadership, leaving the Pashtuns more divided and fractious than ever. In this environment, it is hard to forge consensus, find leaders to work with who have real power, and form alliances without earning the enmity of rival factions. For Coalition forces, the political fault lines are not clear, and there is constant danger of getting drawn into local feuds. Decades of war have also destroyed what little central government once existed in Afghanistan, leaving Coalition troops to build institutions from scratch.

A strong culture of vengeance exists among the Pashtuns. When airstrikes cause harm to civilians or property, or local fighters and tribal leaders are captured or killed in raids, their relatives and fellow clansmen are sometimes obligated to seek revenge. Doing so is a matter of honor. In any society, indiscriminate violence and overly zealous kill-capture missions are likely to undermine popular support and strengthen the insurgency, but in Afghanistan, these actions present the additional danger of causing entire clans and tribes to declare war on Coalition troops.

Finally, Afghanistan is a desperately poor country, its economy based mostly on subsistence agriculture. Reconstruction funds can go a long way where people have so little. Sometimes, a small well or a few jobs is enough to change the economy of an area or to secure the support of a key village or clan. Yet outside money can also be extremely destabilizing for rural communities that are not used to large influxes of cash.

A Localized Insurgency

Afghanistan's politics and economy are extremely localized. Every area is like a separate country. It is not uncommon for major developments in one area to have little or no effect on places just miles away, or for tactics that worked in one location to fail miserably in villages nearby. Marines and soldiers operating in Afghanistan need to understand their local environment on its own terms and tailor their operations accordingly, with the understanding that conditions vary widely from place to place.

Units followed in this book required considerable autonomy, flexibility, and creativity in order to adapt to the unique conditions in their areas of operations. It was extremely difficult for higher headquarters to develop a full picture of the conditions in remote districts. One had to be there over an extended period to develop even a basic understanding of the environment. In many cases, platoons and companies operated in areas so isolated that conditions were radically different and almost entirely disconnected from the rest of the battalion's area of operations.

These differences help explain why successes could apparently be achieved in some places but not in others. For example, Canadian forces in Dand District, south of Kandahar City, made considerable progress employing sound counterinsurgency techniques. Yet Dand was also a relatively peaceful area dominated by tribes inclined to support the government. In Panjwayi, to the west, the Canadians faced considerable difficulty and lost many soldiers—in part because they employed a more heavy-handed approach, but also because the tribes of the Panjwayi had strong connections to the Taliban and a long history of armed resistance (see Vignette 15).

Sangin District in northern Helmand Province was one of the most dangerous areas of Afghanistan, in part because of early operations by the British, however, much of the problem was the town's unique tribal makeup and the fact that it was a major center for the drug trade. Techniques employed with some success in other parts of Helmand had little effect in Sangin (see Vignette 12).

In Nawa District in central Helmand, the U.S. Marines met with quick success, but efforts in Marjah just a short distance away ran into serious trouble—not because of different tactics, but because Marjah was a different sort of place (see Vignette 2). In the east as well, there were places—such as the Korangal Valley in Kunar Province—where U.S. operations led to violent and intractable situations in some valleys but not others.

In some areas, there was an identifiable leadership to work with; in others no one appeared to be in charge. For example, in Chora District in Uruzgan Province, Dutch forces were able to build relationships with some key tribal leaders, which helped stabilize the area. The Dutch then expanded into the nearby Baluchi Valley only to find that there was no discernible tribal leadership. The area was a hornet's nest of competing Ghilzai clans heavily infiltrated by the Taliban. The area's only prominent leader had been killed in a U.S. raid the year before (see Vignette 13).

In other places, the fighting had almost nothing to do with the Taliban or other groups based in Pakistan; the insurgency was about resistance to outside influence and little else in some valleys in the northeast. This was the case, for example, in the Korangal Valley in Kunar Province, one of the most dangerous places for U.S. forces. Similar motivations drove much of the fighting farther north in Nuristan (see Vignette 8). Pashtun tribes across the south and east have a long and proud history of taking up arms against outsiders of every stripe.

A common thread throughout all the vignettes is the importance of involving the local population, communities, and leaders, as well as existing social, political, and economic structures in what the unit commanders were trying to accomplish. Those units that understood the local situation and involved the residents to greater degrees were often able to reach their objectives with less conflict and fewer casualties. Local approaches worked best.

Navigating the Political Terrain

Insurgency is inherently political; it is about employing organized violence to achieve political objectives. The insurgents in Afghanistan are cunning political operatives. To be effective, small units needed to have an intimate knowledge of the political terrain and the ability to navigate it shrewdly. The more successful units immersed themselves in the complex politics in their areas of operation. They gathered information on tribal and ethnic groups—their viewpoints, interests, disputes, and histories of conflict.

Every district and valley of Afghanistan is an intricate web of locally based tribal and clan rivalries, disputes over land and other resources, and feuds that go back generations. In talking to Coalition forces, village leaders often spoke ill of elders in nearby hamlets. The Taliban took advantage of divisions between clans and power brokers, forming alliances with those who harbored grievances against the government or the Coalition, or whose interests were threatened by the U.S. presence.

Ongoing feuds between clans and tribes mirrored the fighting between insurgents and Coalition troops. It was common to see one clan or tribe ally with the government and U.S. forces, and its rival with the Taliban or other Pakistan-based insurgent groups— much like regional powers during the Cold War who joined the United States or the Soviet Union in order to gain leverage against their neighbors. It was not possible to separate these local-level political dynamics from the insurgency writ large; they were inextricably linked.

One of the unintended consequences of forming deep alliances with local tribal groups or power brokers was that it created suspicion and resentment among other groups who then joined the Taliban to balance the power of their rivals. By taking sides and allying with certain power brokers, the United States alienated others—creating opportunities that the Taliban exploited masterfully.

For example, in the Deh Rashaan Valley in Uruzgan, U.S. and Dutch forces worked closely with Barakzai and Popalzai tribesmen and carried out raids against rival Ghilzai tribes to the north. The Ghilzais in turn allied with the Taliban (see Vignette 14). Of two rival Noorzai Pashtun clans in Gulistan in southwest Afghanistan, the militarily weaker but better educated clan latched onto the Marines when they arrived in the spring of 2008; the other kept its ties to the Taliban (see Vignette 1).

In Deh Rawood District in Uruzgan Province, rival factions tried constantly to use their access to Coalition troops as leverage against their local enemies. U.S. forces had allied with local strongmen, prompting others to ally with the Taliban and fire on U.S. troops. The Dutch faced fewer attacks in part because they made neutrality a core objective (see Vignette 13).

Through these experiences, units learned that it was essential to remain neutral in local conflicts and to be seen as an honest broker and a fair provider of public goods, such as security and infrastructure. Doing so required not taking sides or getting involved in feuds between tribes and clans and not forming alliances of any sort. Military officers had to understand the politics and be involved in them to some extent but also had to remain above the fray and unassociated with any particular faction—a very difficult thing to do.

Searching for Political Solutions

The most successful operations were those in which a unit identified the political problems driving the insurgency in its area and came up with viable solutions. In these cases, further counterinsurgency operations were sometimes unnecessary. Dialogue and negotiation also reduced the amount of fighting necessary during clear-hold-build operations and helped protect vulnerable forces in isolated areas.

For example, in the Mirabad Valley in Uruzgan Province, a place notorious for improvised explosive devices (IEDs) detonated against Dutch forces, a mobile battle group of British marines pushed in, met with the valley's elders, and determined that the people of the Mirabad had allied with the Taliban as a result of repeated abuses by the district police chief and the men under his command. The valley's leaders also felt they had been shut out of power at the provincial level and that rival tribes were using their control over the government to exploit the people of the Mirabad.

The British marines persuaded the Dutch to reach out to the valley's leaders, bring them into the political process in the provincial capital, fire the police chief, and rein in the local police. Soon thereafter, the IEDs in the Mirabad Valley disappeared, and the Dutch were able to move through the valley unmolested. The valley was stabilized without any permanent deployment of forces and without firing a shot. Once the various parties had reached a political solution, further action, including clear-hold-build operations, was no longer required (see Vignette 11).

Reaching out to marginalized groups proved effective elsewhere as well. For example, U.S. soldiers in the northeast made a point of engaging with Nuristani clans left out of power at the district and provincial levels. Evidently, earlier units deployed to this region had not dealt with these clans, many of which were responsible for attacks on U.S. forces. Attacks on convoys in the region dropped significantly once U.S. forces engaged with these marginalized tribes (see Vignette 4).

Political engagement lent legitimacy to combat operations and allowed units to achieve military objectives with less fighting and loss of life. For example, as the British prepared to retake the town of Musa Qala in northern Helmand in 2007, they established contact with a prominent tribal leader whose fighters made up the bulk of the Taliban force there. The British persuaded the leader to defect in exchange for political power once the British took over. As the UK-led task force moved on the town, the leader ordered his fellow tribesmen to stand down. The remaining insurgents melted away with little fighting as the Coalition swept into the town (see Vignette 10).

In Nuristan, a battalion of U.S. soldiers was able to project power into some of the most dangerous and hostile terrain in all of Afghanistan by negotiating with village leaders ahead of military operations. Unlike earlier units deployed to Nuristan, the battalion faced relatively little resistance as it pushed into isolated mountain valleys that had a long history of armed resistance against outsiders—valleys where there had been numerous attacks on U.S. forces in the past. After months of painstaking talks with the elders of eastern Nuristan, the battalion was able to negotiate a peace between U.S. forces, village leaders, and the insurgents. These negotiations allowed the battalion to push into the area without a shot being fired. These negotiations required substantial knowledge about the political terrain and considerable diplomatic skills (see Vignette 4).

Engaging the Population and Building Popular Support

Soldiers and Marines who used a population-centered approach tended to make more progress with less violence than those who focused on the enemy or the terrain. Doing so required dispersing into small outposts in or near populated areas, getting out constantly on foot, engaging and collaborating with local leaders, and implementing development projects that benefitted communities and built popular support. Units that followed this approach took on greater risk in the short term, but usually ended up safer in the long run.

The more successful units focused almost entirely on the population. Many did not bother to chase down insurgents. When the Marines cleared through Nawa in 2009, they focused on setting up outposts and beginning reconstruction. They allowed many fighters to escape and even offered amnesty to those who agreed to lay down their arms (see Vignette 2).

On the few occasions that Afghan National Army (ANA) units led clear-hold-build operations, they too focused on the population and did not give chase to fleeing insurgents. For example, in the Tagab Valley east of Kabul, Afghan soldiers did not even shoot back when fired upon. Instead, they moved slowly up the valley, holding *shuras* (meetings of local leaders) in villages, setting up bases, and starting reconstruction projects. The Afghan army managed to stabilize the valley with little fighting (see Vignette 3).

Using Afghan forces to engage the population helped build relationships. Military operations that included local security forces were more effective than those that involved only Coalition troops. Even more so, when U.S. advisors were embedded with the Afghan army—not just occasionally conducting operations with them—the effects were more positive. In many places, the local population was more willing to accept the presence of Afghan soldiers, and they attracted fewer attacks (see Vignette 3).

Successful counterinsurgency operations involved constant interaction with local people and countless cups of tea and sociable conversation. Relationship building proved essential. Afghanistan, like most underdeveloped rural nations, is a relationship-based society. In such places, building trust is necessary, which takes time, commitment, and work. It was not enough to institutionalize interactions between commanding officers and government officials—personal rapport was crucial.

Conducting foot patrols from small outposts in populated areas also proved essential. On foot, soldiers and Marines were able to interact with people constantly in order to gather useful information and understanding and to form relationships. Small units that spread out into small outposts and patrolled every day on foot were more effective than large units that were consolidated on large bases disconnected from the local population (see Vignettes 2, 5, 13, and 14).

Armored vehicles and large, heavily fortified bases put barriers between local people and Coalition troops. The same was true of wearing body armor and carrying weapons— and especially pointing guns at civilians. In 2003, when permissive security conditions in Kandahar City allowed U.S. troops to drive in unarmored vehicles and walk around without guns or body armor, it was much easier to engage with the people. As violence grew in later years and the Coalition shifted to battle mode, Coalition troops became increasingly cut off from the city's population (see Vignette 9).

Units that projected a heavier, more imposing and invasive presence often attracted more attacks. The more successful special forces teams operating in remote areas learned that it was important to maintain a light footprint in order to gain access to the population; otherwise, a team's actions could threaten local power brokers and heavily armed clans that had a penchant for taking up arms against outsiders. Providing a nonintrusive benefit won local support and therefore local protection. Leveraging Afghan leaders to mobilize the population often proved to be the best way to defeat the insurgency. The worst possible outcome for Coalition troops in Afghanistan was to be seen as an army of occupation (see Vignette 4).

Foot patrols and engagement with the population also saved lives. In Kandahar Province, for example, Canadian soldiers in such districts as Zharey and Panjwayi operated out of large, heavily fortified bases and moved around in armored vehicles. These units met with intense fighting and took many casualties. In areas where the Canadians dispersed onto small bases and patrolled on foot, they suffered fewer attacks (see Vignette 15).

The same was true for the U.S. Marines in Nawa in 2009. They spread out into 26 small outposts and conducted constant foot patrols out of these bases. They were out so often that the locals wondered whether the Marines ever slept. They also held shuras nearly every day near their outposts. By doing so, the Marines in Nawa were able to dominate the areas around their positions and build support among the nearby population (see Vignette 2).

In Helmand and parts of Kandahar, the insurgents used IEDs to prevent Coalition troops from interacting with the people. The aim of the IEDs was to make movement so dangerous that soldiers and Marines would no longer patrol far from their bases, ceding control over the population to the Taliban. In most cases, the best counter to the IED threat was regular foot patrols and engagement with the population.

Soldiers and Marines who were able to build support among the population found that the IED threat diminished considerably over time. On the other hand, the more troops stayed in their bases and allowed their movements to be restricted, the more intense the IED threat became. This was the case in many places, including Sangin, the notorious town in northern Helmand where thousands of IEDs stood between British forces and the population (see Vignette 12).

In many remote areas, the population protected U.S. and NATO forces—not the other way around, as is suggested by the counterinsurgency manual. For many of the 12-man special forces teams operating out of isolated firebases, building a base of support among the local population was essential for survival. Popular support, gained through sound counterinsurgency techniques, proved to be the best form of force protection. In some places, special forces teams moved safely in areas with substantial Taliban presence because the local population supported the team's presence and pledged to protect it from attack (see Vignette 7).

The same was often true of conventional forces stationed in remote and dangerous areas. For example, soldiers in northern Kunar and eastern Nuristan managed to befriend village leaders who offered sanctuary to U.S. forces passing through. These leaders also promised protection to U.S. troops when within the confines of their villages. Local elders sometimes accompanied U.S. Army patrols outside their villages in order to deter attacks by local militants. These patrols were rarely, if ever, fired upon (see Vignette 4).

However, not far away in the Korangal Valley, where the population was hostile and village leaders refused sanctuary to U.S. forces, soldiers were under constant fire everywhere and took many casualties. Where Coalition troops had popular support, they faced little danger; where they were looked upon as an occupying force, they were never secure, even in the apparently safe confines of their bases.

Using Reconstruction Funds

Many units learned to target their use of reconstruction funds toward specific objectives rather than fund projects for their own sake. This meant using funds to gain and maintain support in key areas, draw fighting-age males away from the insurgency, bring quarrelling factions to the negotiating table, and punish recalcitrant tribes and clans.

It was not enough to simply execute a large number of reconstruction projects—to give people wells, roads, and other amenities in the hope of winning hearts and minds. Throwing money at problems rarely worked. Successful units used reconstruction funds to build relationships in pursuit of clear political objectives. These relationships were often more important than the projects themselves.

Used unwisely, reconstruction funds frequently did more harm than good. For example, it was not uncommon for resentful tribes who did not receive funds to sabotage projects and attack U.S. troops. Contractors who became wealthy and powerful as a result of their special relationship with U.S. forces threatened local power brokers, leading to violence that was often mistaken for insurgent activity. The same was true of projects that employed outside labor.

Those units that were able to tie the local economy into the continued presence of Coalition forces were particularly successful. They did this mainly by creating jobs and targeting certain leaders or segments of the population. The goal was to bring money into the community without upsetting the political and social balance of the locality. This worked even where the population was inclined to support the insurgency (see Vignette 7).

Reconstruction projects aimed at large-scale job creation tended to be effective, especially where there were large numbers of landless laborers. For example, Canadian engineers in Dand District, south of Kandahar City, recognized early on that a few wealthy men owned all the land. Nearly everyone living in the district were sharecroppers and laborers who stood to gain little from roads, irrigation canals, wells, and other projects that promised to improve the productivity of the land. Such projects would merely enrich a few large landowners. The Canadians instead focused on low-technology, labor-intensive projects aimed at providing jobs to young men of fighting age. After six months, the Taliban was no longer able to recruit fighters in Dand District (see Vignette 15).

When it came to getting results from job creation programs, much depended on local conditions. For example, like the Canadians in Kandahar, U.S. soldiers in northeast Afghanistan focused on low-technology projects aimed at providing employment. Yet insurgent facilitators based in Pakistan offered generous salaries to would-be recruits— far more than the U.S. military could provide with its limited amount of funds. Reconstruction projects in the northeast did not yield the clear-cut results that Canadian soldiers saw south of Kandahar City (see Vignette 4). In Sangin in northern Helmand, a major center for the poppy trade, well-heeled drug traffickers (who were allied with the Taliban) paid handsomely for attacks on British forces. The funds available to the drug traffickers dwarfed those available to British forces (see Vignette 12).

Successful units recognized that money was power. U.S. soldiers in Zabul's Shinkay Valley dispensed funds as patronage—much like a patronage-based political machine. They used their money to create a network of supporters around their firebase and in villages farther beyond. Successful units gave money directly to laborers, rather than go through local contractors or power brokers, unless their intention was to empower these individuals (see Vignette 7).

They also spread their funds around in order to avoid the appearance of favoritism that might breed resentment. In Dand District, the Canadians hired one fighting-age male from every extended family. Their intention was to spread their funds out as evenly as possible and to tie every family in the district into the reconstruction effort. (see Vignette 15)

In northeast Afghanistan, U.S soldiers gave funds directly to village leaders in exchange for specific concessions, such as support for upcoming operations, actionable intelligence, or reduced attacks on convoys. In this case, the battalion's objectives were to empower cooperative local leaders by giving them control over reconstruction funds and to give the battalion leverage over these leaders. The soldiers also pushed money into outlying areas ahead of major operations in order to buy support and soften resistance. This approach worked well and saved many lives (see Vignette 4).

In Nangarhar Province in the east, U.S. forces supported a governor who paid tribal leaders to stop growing poppy. The governor combined these incentives with threats against those who refused to comply. In just one year, Nangarhar went from being one of Afghanistan's main opium cultivators to one that was declared "poppy free." (see Vignette 6)

Raising and Advising Indigenous Forces

Building soldiers, police,[*] and irregular forces was an essential but often overlooked mission. At the strategic level, the effort was disorganized and poorly resourced. It was not until relatively late in the conflict—when U.S. commanders began thinking about drawing down—that raising indigenous forces became a priority and the effort began to pick up steam. Despite these problems, Army and Marine training teams made a great deal of progress at the tactical level, especially advising Afghan soldiers, standing up local police, and using irregular forces.

The more successful training teams were embedded with Afghan units at every level. These teams lived with the Afghan soldiers and police. They patrolled with them, fought with them, and sometimes died with them. Afghan security forces went through training in regional academies, but the training they received in the field from embedded advisors was key. In many cases, the presence of combat mentors kept Afghan units together and allowed them to go on patrol and carry out operations. Embedded advisors were the steel frame that kept Afghan forces operational until they gained enough experience to operate on their own. This model of combat advising was far more effective than partnering, in which U.S. units carried out joint operations with Afghan forces.

Combat advising was one of the most difficult and dangerous missions in Afghanistan. Trainers moved around with Afghan units, often in convoys of soft-skinned vehicles that did not have dedicated air support or quick reaction forces. They went on missions with

---

* For more on police advisors in Afghanistan, see William Rosenau, *Acknowledging Limits: Police Advisors and Counterinsurgency in Afghanistan* (Quantico, VA: Marine Corps University Press, 2011).

Afghan soldiers and police who did not speak English, did not always stand their ground when engaged, were not well armed or equipped, and who could not always be trusted.

For example, in Gulistan District in southwest Afghanistan in early 2008, a platoon of U.S. Marines was tasked with building a local police force whose chief was working for the Taliban. The police chief informed on the Marines for the Taliban and tried to lead the Marines into pre-laid ambushes. The police chief arranged for the killing of his own men if they refused to cooperate with the insurgents. Not until the Marines pushed the Taliban out of the area were they able to turn the police force around (see Vignette 1).

In 2008, Afghan army units, assisted by U.S. Marine trainers embedded at multiple levels of command, cleared through the insurgent-controlled Tagab Valley in central Afghanistan and built a solid base of support among the population. With the assistance of their combat advisors, the Afghan army took responsibility over battlespace for the first time since the U.S. intervention in 2001. When given the support they needed—and left to their own devices and not overshadowed by larger U.S. forces—these Afghan units did quite well (see Vignette 3).

In places where the Taliban was particularly strong, combat advisors kept Afghan army units from crumbling in the face of constant ambushes and IEDs. British advisors in Sangin in Helmand Province lived with Afghan army units on small bases and patrolled with them daily (see Vignette 12). U.S. Marines followed this model when they took over British-controlled areas in southern Afghanistan (see Vignette 2). Where there was hard fighting, it was absolutely essential that Afghan units received the support they needed; when they did not, units quickly deteriorated. Embedded advisors from U.S. and NATO militaries were instrumental in ensuring that Afghan soldiers and police received adequate support, especially when under attack.

U.S. and NATO forces also made good use of local security guards and irregular forces. For example, U.S. soldiers in the remote northeastern mountains learned that the insurgents were more reluctant to fire on local Afghan guards. Posting locals at guard posts led to a reduction in attacks on U.S. bases in Kunar and Nuristan Provinces. American soldiers also persuaded local leaders to protect reconstruction projects in their villages (see Vignette 4). Special forces teams in Kunar organized local defense forces to protect road projects and held local leaders responsible for attacks on these projects near their villages (see Vignette 8).

Protecting the Population

Preventing the insurgents from intimidating the population was essential to building popular support and making reconstruction work. Afghans were rarely willing to cooperate with Coalition troops if they (or their families) believed they might face retaliation. Where insurgents could target individuals working with the Coalition, the presence of Coalition troops did more harm than good. In contested areas where Coalition forces and insurgents fought for control over the same population, the plight of civilians was the worst.

Where the insurgents managed to infiltrate back into cleared areas and operate underground, reconstruction efforts faltered or failed altogether. For example, in such places as Nawa and Musa Qala in Helmand, U.S. and British forces managed to push the insurgents out and keep them from returning. In these places, the population cooperated with the Coalition, and reconstruction efforts proved relatively successful (see Vignettes 2 and 10). In other areas of Helmand, such as Marjah and Sangin, where the insurgents infiltrated back in to intimidate the population and lay IEDs and ambushes, U.S. and British forces faced considerable difficulties with rebuilding the government and getting projects underway (see Vignette 12). In such places, the population was often less secure and less well-governed than under the Taliban. People played both sides in order to survive.

In many places where insurgent influence remained strong, soldiers and Marines could not trust local government officials, especially the police. For example, in Gulistan in early 2008, a U.S. Marine platoon was forced to work with a district governor and police chief who were actively collaborating with the Taliban. The government officials tried to lure the Marines into pre-laid ambushes and reportedly engineered the killing of local police who cooperated with the platoon. Only when the Marines succeeded in pushing the Taliban out of most parts of the valley—thereby ending its campaign of intimidation—did district officials start cooperating with the Marines (see Vignette 1).

Many Afghans were skeptical about the commitment of U.S. and NATO units. Local people had to consider their lives and those of their families five or more years down the road when the Taliban might very well return to power and retaliate against those who had collaborated with the Coalition (see Vignettes 2 and 14).

In some areas, the population did not want the protection of Coalition troops or Afghan soldiers. Permanent garrisons and checkpoints attracted insurgent attacks and led to fighting that caused harm to civilian life and property. In some of the more remote areas, Taliban influence was relatively benign; violent struggles for control between insurgents and Coalition troops posed a greater threat (see Vignette 7).

Employing Restraint in the Use of Force

Restraint in the use of force was essential to every operation detailed in this book. Killing the wrong people had far-reaching consequences. In many places, ill-informed or poorly conceived combat operations reversed months—and in some cases, years— worth of patient effort overnight. In other places, targeting operations had second-order effects that were not apparent until months or years later.

Power brokers close to U.S. forces often used their special relationships with the Coalition to eliminate their enemies by passing false information naming their rivals as Taliban. Officers repeatedly fell for these tricks, carrying out raids against individuals based on information from local interlocutors whose motives were questionable. These operations—in which U.S. and NATO units were manipulated into killing prominent local leaders whose commitment to the insurgency was uncertain—created powerful enemies and probably caused more harm than had they done nothing at all.

For example, in the Deh Rashaan Valley north of Tarin Kowt, the Ghilzai clans in the northern part of the valley allied with the Taliban after a series of airstrikes by U.S. and Australian forces that killed several prominent tribal leaders. Their rivals among the Popalzai and Barakzai to the south—who controlled the provincial government and had regular access to Coalition forces—may have identified certain Ghilzai leaders as Taliban, when in fact their connections to the movement were tenuous and uncertain. Rather than reach out to the Ghilzai clans and try to bring them into the government, Coalition troops targeted their leaders for assassination, alienating and pushing them into alliances with the Taliban, which deepened the divide further and led to more violence (see Vignette 14).

Generally, killing people, even insurgents, did more harm than good. Many insurgents were related to locals, including prominent leaders working with the government and U.S. forces. Killing locals often fueled demands for vengeance, even if these young men were obviously involved in the insurgency. Many local residents resented the killing of their loved ones no matter what their activities might have been. In many cases, avenging their deaths was a matter of honor, and it was common for clans targeted in earlier raids to attack U.S. and NATO forces of their own accord (see Vignettes 4, 8, and 14).

Military units that were successful at stabilizing an area and building popular support almost never carried out raids in populated areas they sought to influence. For example, Dutch soldiers in Uruzgan did not conduct raids in or near the areas where they intended to build popular support (see Vignette 13). The same was true of some special forces teams (see Vignette 7).

Raids against enemy fighters tended to yield mixed results. In many cases, they proved counterproductive—especially in remote, mountainous areas where there were few Coalition forces and little accurate and up-to-date information. In the mountains, the terrain was so difficult, the road infrastructure so limited, and the distances so long that insurgent leaders often had plenty of time to flee, leaving innocent people to suffer the consequences of Coalition attacks. It was nearly impossible for outside forces to move through the mountains undetected (see Vignette 8). Air assault raids in particular were a problem because most of the forces carrying out these operations were based far from their targets and knew little about the areas in which they operated (see Vignette 7).

It was not uncommon for villagers to take up arms against outsiders—any outsiders, whether rival clans or U.S. forces—who entered the confines of their villages uninvited, especially at night. Under such circumstances, Coalition troops could not easily distinguish between insurgents trying to protect themselves and local men seeking to defend their village. Many units simply assumed that anyone firing at them was an enemy fighter. Raids in which innocent people were harmed or their honor violated created enduring enmity in many areas of the country. As a result, entire families, clans, or even tribes took up arms against the Coalition and allied with the Taliban (see Vignette 7).

In several cases covered in this book, kill-capture missions and other enemy-centric combat operations caused violence to escalate significantly. For example, security conditions in Kandahar City in 2003 were so permissive that Coalition troops walked around without body armor. Later units focused on raids and measured their progress by the number of enemy fighters killed. As a result, Kandahar City became increasingly violent and unstable, and relations between U.S. forces and the population grew strained (see Vignette 9).

These vicious cycles strengthened the insurgency and created problems that became increasingly difficult to solve. Misplaced combat operations caused entire clans or tribes to declare war on Coalition forces, prompting the shedding of more blood and demands for more vengeance. Killing more people often made the problem worse and gave strength to the insurgency.

Large-scale sweep operations in particular were ineffective and counterproductive. These operations, which involved a battalion or more of U.S. forces pushing into a large area from different directions in order to kill or capture a substantial number of insurgents, caused significant damage to civilian life and property yet netted few enemy fighters. Most of these sweeps were slow, clumsy, and ill-informed. Insurgents easily escaped through porous cordons or hid their weapons and pretended to be civilians. Since holding forces were rarely left behind, the insurgents returned to business as usual when the operations were over. Afghan militia forces involved in these operations were often accused of widespread looting. These operations alienated entire valleys, causing untold damage to the overall U.S. effort (see Vignette 7).

Despite these pitfalls, the discriminate use of force was often an integral part of counterinsurgency in Afghanistan. The goal was to demonstrate superior strength and will to the insurgents and the population while doing no harm to civilian life or property. After decades of civil war in which villages had seen one armed faction after another take power, many Afghans had learned to support whichever side happened to be the strongest.

For example, when the U.S. Marines arrived in Gulistan in southwest Afghanistan in the spring of 2008, they encountered a population that was almost entirely controlled by the Taliban. Most villages initially expressed indifference or outright hostility toward the Marines. After a number of high-profile engagements where the Marines prevailed without hurting civilians or their property, entire villages began working with them (see Vignette 1). In Nawa in central Helmand, the Marines defeated the Taliban in a matter of days. Once it was clear that the insurgents stood no chance—and that the Marines were there to stay—the population turned around almost immediately (see Vignette 2).

Restraint was usually the better part of valor, and diplomacy was more important than force. The insurgents exploited local grievances to build popular support and recruit fighters. Killing insurgents often aggravated these grievances, made political solutions more difficult, and expanded the pool of enemy fighters. In the words of one battalion commander in northeast Afghanistan, "You can't simply kill your way out of an insurgency. The supply of fighters here is inexhaustible" (see Vignette 4).

Some of the vignettes in this book suggest that it may never be too late to turn the tide. Often, officers were able to reach out to leaders whose communities had been victims of heavy-handed operations to offer compensation and promise that past mistakes would not be repeated. In Kunar, a U.S. Army battalion made peace with an openly hostile village that had been the site of several botched raids during earlier years of the war. The village had since become the site of numerous attacks on U.S. forces. Through public apologies, sustained engagement, reconstruction projects, and assurances that all future raids would cease, the battalion was able to turn the village around. Attacks stopped, and insurgents were no longer able to operate there (see Vignette 4).

Finding the Right Balance Between Concentration and Dispersion

It took time and a lot of trial and error for units to figure out how much territory and how much of the population they could reasonably control with the capabilities they had. Finding the right balance between concentration and dispersion—in order to adequately protect the population and limit insurgent safe areas without spreading one's forces too thin—was particularly hard in Afghanistan, with its vast expanses of rural hinterland, unforgiving terrain, and spread-out population.

Where a large number of forces were deployed in a relatively small area— such as the U.S. Marines in Helmand after 2008—the dilemma was less acute. But where small units were responsible for massive areas, no good solutions could be found. There were always areas of Afghanistan's vast rural hinterland where the Taliban could operate safely, and that created pressure for U.S. and NATO forces to constantly clear new areas. Once there, they could not withdraw. Otherwise, the Taliban would return and the gains made would quickly disappear.

Some battalions were spread out across an entire province, or even multiple provinces. For example, 2d Battalion, 7th Marines (2/7), the first U.S. Marine unit to establish a permanent presence in southern Afghanistan, was spread across eight districts in Helmand and Farah Provinces. Many of the routes between bases passed through Taliban-controlled territory. The 2/7 was ordered to train the police in each of these eight districts, forcing the battalion to disperse its forces across a massive area mostly controlled by the Taliban (see Vignette 1).

In eastern Afghanistan in 2007 and 2008, a U.S. Army battalion was responsible for all of northern Kunar and eastern Nuristan. The battalion operated across multiple mountain ranges, its forces dispersed into combat outposts that could only be reached by air (see Vignette 4). Before 2007, a single 12-man U.S. Army Special Forces team was responsible for this entire region (see Vignette 8). Army Special Forces teams elsewhere in Afghanistan were responsible for similarly large areas (see Vignette 7).

Some Coalition troops were able to follow a gradualist, oil-spot strategy that involved focusing on small areas where they knew they could make a difference, rather than rapidly expanding into new areas. These units met with greater success, at least in the areas where they focused their energies. The oil-spot approach, which involved protecting and consolidating a base of support and then slowly expanding this base, seemed to work better than rapid expansion through large-scale clearing operations.

For example, in Dand District south of Kandahar City, a reinforced company of Canadian soldiers and engineers focused on only one village at first. Once this village and its immediate surroundings were stable, the soldiers slowly expanded into nearby villages (see Vignette 15). The Dutch followed a similar approach in Uruzgan Province. In areas where the Dutch focused their energies, they met with considerable success (see Vignette 13).

The downside of the oil-spot approach was that it left many areas under de facto Taliban rule. For example, the Dutch followed an oil-spot strategy that involved focusing on small areas where they knew they could make a difference, recognizing that the Taliban would continue to operate further afield. Though Dutch influence in Uruzgan remained strong in certain areas, the Taliban operated freely in much of the province.

The initial British plan in 2006 was to oil spot out from Helmand's provincial capital, Lashkar Gah, but when the Taliban attacked all of the towns in northern Helmand simultaneously, the British were forced to fan out across the province in order to keep the majority of Helmand's population from falling under Taliban control. The British soon found themselves spread thin, under siege, and unable to conduct patrols and engage effectively with the population. Because they were so spread out, the insurgents were able to infiltrate back into many cleared areas. This was true for many U.S. units as well.

Many units learned the hard way the perils of expanding too far too soon. In many cases, they did not know what they were getting into. The insurgents' strength only became apparent once new areas had been cleared, new bases set up, and new commitments made. Returning to a more consolidated force posture required shutting down bases under duress, which looked a lot like defeat.

Units that went too far afield or spread out across too large an area found their lines of communication frequently cut, their smaller bases and outposts under threat, and their influence attenuated. This was a serious problem for the British in southern Afghanistan in 2006 and 2007 and was also a problem for the U.S. forces in eastern Afghanistan with its high mountains and long distances. In the northeast, insurgents actually overran two remote bases—Combat Outposts Wanat and Keating—in 2008 and 2009.

Was it better to focus on a smaller area in the hopes of making solid gains there or to cast a wide net hoping to put pressure on the Taliban everywhere? In Afghanistan, with its unforgiving terrain and spread-out population, there was never a good answer to this question.

The only real solution to this dilemma was to build Afghan security forces capable of protecting the population in newly cleared areas. Coalition troops, however, rarely did so.

Only in one vignette—in which Afghan soldiers supported by U.S. Marine advisors stabilized an insurgent-controlled valley east of Kabul—was this approach adopted. Another rarely tried solution was mobilizing the population and integrating local defense forces with national forces. The police, which often served as de facto paramilitaries charged with fighting the insurgents rather than policing the population, did not have the capability or professionalism to hold back the Taliban on their own.

Maintaining Continuity

The counterinsurgency effort in Afghanistan suffered from constant unit turnover, lack of historical memory, and a tendency to repeat mistakes. Units on their way out took much of their hard-won local knowledge with them. In most cases, new units had to "reinvent the wheel." In some areas, local Afghans had seen 10 to 15 units cycle through, each a blank slate.

Relationships between Coalition forces and local Afghans suffered every time units rotated out and new ones took their place. For example, in Khost Province, the battalion commander and provincial reconstruction team commander built strong relationships with the governor and other officials; their subordinate officers built similar relationships with other officials across the province. Popular support for the United States grew in Khost and violence dropped off. Yet, when the battalion left and a new group of officers came in, relationships frayed. Insurgents exploited the situation with a surge in attacks, and the progress achieved quickly disappeared (see Vignette 5).

The gains made with the population were often fragile. It was not uncommon for a unit to make considerable progress, only to see those gains disappear or even reverse themselves a year or two later. For example, Khost Province in 2007 was dubbed a model of effective counterinsurgency by many, including the Afghan president and U.S. secretary of defense. A year later, violence again escalated when the insurgents went on the offensive, relationships between key figures broke down, and much of what had been accomplished in 2006 and 2007 was quickly erased (see Vignette 5). U.S. Army Special Forces teams in Kandahar faced similar problems: gains made in Kandahar in 2003 were wiped out in 2004 by new units that focused on kill-capture missions and allowed relationships with local people to falter (see Vignette 9).

Such radical shifts in focus from one unit to the next sent mixed messages to the population. They signaled a lack of determination and commitment that U.S. efforts would be sustained. Local people began to hedge their bets and collaborate with the Taliban.

Forging Unity of Effort Without Unity of Command

The more successful counterinsurgency operations were those in which different units and government agencies worked closely together at the local level. Doing so was not easy in the absence of a unified command structure. Special forces units, officials from the State Department and USAID, conventional forces, and civilian and military personnel from different NATO countries all had separate reporting chains. Even basic communication was a challenge.

Units that failed to coordinate often operated at cross-purposes. This problem was especially acute where commando units were engaged in counterterrorist operations in the same areas that conventional forces were focused on counterinsurgency. It was not uncommon for kill-capture teams to carry out raids in the same villages where conventional forces were attempting to build popular support. Some of these raids were based on faulty intelligence, resulting in the deaths of innocent village leaders. Others caused collateral damage that angered the population, undercutting months of painstaking effort. It often took years for conventional forces to regain support in these areas.

In Khost Province, the Army battalion, provincial reconstruction team (PRT), and special forces units worked closely together. The battalion worked with the commandos to limit night raids in certain areas and to increase the accuracy of the intelligence on which these raids were based. The PRT engaged with local leaders, some of whom provided actionable information and willingly handed over suspected insurgent leaders and facilitators. This cooperation broke down with the arrival of new unit commanders (see Vignette 5).

Civil-military coordination was key in areas with multiple units. For example, in Nangarhar Province, the Army battalion, provincial reconstruction team, agribusiness development unit, and counternarcotics team worked together to support the governor's plan to eliminate opium poppy from the province. The effort was a success, due in large part to effective coordination and the use of reconstruction funds toward the same goals (see Vignette 6).

Unfortunately, such unity of effort was more the exception than the rule. Without unity of command, the level of coordination depended heavily on the personalities of different commanders. With the rotation of each new unit, relationships had to be rebuilt between different U.S. and NATO partners, and between American and Afghan officials. It was not uncommon for cooperation to break down due to personality conflicts, differences in opinion, or lack of communication. With such a fragmented command structure, no leadership at the top was capable of enforcing unity among units in the field.

Operating with Little Strategic Guidance

In most of the cases outlined in this book, units that followed a population-centric approach did so of their own initiative, in response to local conditions, and with little strategic guidance. Many mission statements said little more than "conduct COIN" or "target insurgents," leaving it up to the small unit on the ground to figure out what objectives it should have and how to achieve them.

The vignettes in this book suggest that there was a lack of clear direction and unity of effort at the top until at least mid-2009. Campaign plans and strategy documents existed, but they were often contradictory and not stringently enforced or clearly communicated. For every unit that focused on the population, others did not. Operations at the tactical and operational levels were not nested within a single strategic framework. Units often worked at cross-purposes and approaches changed from one commander to the next. As a result, many hard-won gains were lost.

That said, deeper forces were also at work that militated against the development of a clear strategy—and will continue to do so in the future. Conditions in Afghanistan vary so widely and forces are so thinly spread out that operations are by necessity extremely localized. In such an environment, offering clear and relevant strategic direction from the top—from a headquarters hundreds of miles away across some of the world's most impassable terrain—is an enormous challenge. The Afghan leadership in Kabul faces similar challenges when it comes to managing district governments.

Even the most focused and carefully formulated strategy will run into problems in such an environment. At the end of the day, it will be up to small unit leaders to adapt counterinsurgency principles to the unique circumstances in their areas of operation.

The vignettes that follow describe some of the conditions faced by small units in re-mote regions of Afghanistan, the approaches they adopted, and some of the successes they achieved. They demonstrate what can be accomplished at the local level, even in the absence of clear strategic guidance.

U.S. Marine Platoon
Gulistan, Farah, 2008

From May to November 2008, a platoon of U.S. Marines from 2d Battalion, 7th Marine Regiment (2/7) operated in the isolated and dangerous Gulistan Valley in Farah Province in southwest Afghanistan. Gulistan District was an enemy sanctuary that had never been pacified. The insurgents had a firm hold on the population, the district government, and police. By November, the platoon of Marines had pushed the Taliban out of the district's main villages and built a base of support for the government.

The 2d Battalion, 7th Marines was the first U.S. Marine battalion to establish a permanent presence in southern Afghanistan. Its mission was to train the Afghan police in eight districts in northern Helmand and Farah, a vast, mostly ungoverned area where insurgents moved freely. After arriving in theater, the battalion learned that there were few functioning police forces in these districts and that the area was almost entirely controlled by the Taliban.

Gulistan was the most remote district in 2/7's area of operations. The platoon's outpost was located more than a day's drive from the nearest U.S. base. A few U.S. and NATO units had been in and out of Gulistan, but none had established a permanent presence. These forces had achieved little and built few relationships with the locals.

Establishing the Marines' Footprint in Gulistan

In April 2008, 2d Battalion was sent to southwest Afghanistan to train the local police. The battalion was spread across eight districts in two provinces straddling two regional commands. In Helmand Province, the battalion was responsible for the districts of Musa Qala, Sangin, Now Zad, and Washir. In Farah Province, the battalion had Bala Baluk, Bakwa, Delaram, and Gulistan Districts.

Unless otherwise noted, information in this vignette comes from interviews with the platoon commander on 13 May 2010.

Forward Operating Base Gulistan on 8 July 2008. (Photo by LCpl Gene Allen Ainsworth III, U.S. Marine Corps)

This vast area consisted of large numbers of highly proficient Taliban fighters and virtually no competent police. British forces in Sangin, Musa Qala, and Now Zad were under constant siege. In six of these districts, the Marines were the only significant military force (British forces were in Sangin and Musa Qala); it was up to them to hold these districts against the Taliban while building police forces from scratch. The Marines' deployment was meant to be a one-shot effort with no plan for follow-on forces, yet the battalion ended up establishing what would become a long-term U.S. Marine presence in Farah and northern Helmand.

Within weeks of arriving in theater, the battalion was ordered to disperse its three rifle companies across this vast area. One company was sent to Sangin, another to Musa Qala and Now Zad. The third went to Delaram, a notorious truck stop along the Ring Road between Helmand and Farah Provinces. This third company was responsible for four districts in Farah, all Taliban sanctuary areas.

In late May, a platoon of Marines left Delaram and drove north into the remote Gulistan Valley. The platoon set up a makeshift combat outpost at the district center next to the local boys' school and met with local officials. Armed only with some basic maps, many of them dating back to the 1950s, the Marines knew almost nothing about the area.

They also did not know before they arrived that Gulistan District was entirely under the control of the insurgents who collected taxes and operated a parallel shadow government. It was common knowledge in the valley that the district governor and police chief were actively collaborating with the Taliban, which ruled through a combination of political alliances and intimidation. Militants from Helmand and other areas of Afghanistan used Gulistan as a safe haven—a place to rest, train, and plan operations.

The platoon's combat outpost, located at the district center, was a day's drive from the company headquarters in Delaram, through mountain passes controlled by the insurgents. In October 2007, more than 100 insurgents from Helmand had launched a catastrophic ambush on a U.S.-Afghan convoy attempting to regain control over the valley. Before the Marines arrived, the small district police garrison had been repeatedly overrun.

As soon as the Marines arrived, the Taliban stepped up its campaign of intimidation. Within days of the platoon's arrival, the Americans observed a car driving through the village. As the vehicle passed down the main road in the village, people turned off their lights and generators. The Marines learned the next morning that the car was that of a Taliban commander threatening people with beatings or death if they played music, allowed women to leave the home, sent their girls to school, or interacted with the Marines.

The Taliban delivered "night letters" (written threats delivered under the cover of darkness) to a nearby girls' school, forcing it to shut down. The Marines countered with security patrols and a mobile defense of the schoolhouse during the school day. Within two weeks the school was running again. The insurgents also threatened the police, most of whom were local men with families living in the valley. There were daily reports that insurgents were organizing to attack the platoon's combat outpost.

The district governor and police chief actively collaborated with the Taliban. Although they were from different clans, they were close allies. These officials fed the Marines false information and sold weapons and ammunition to the insurgents.

The Taliban continued to control the only route into and out of the valley, through the Buji Bast Pass, south of the district center. In mid-June, the Marines surrounded a village near the pass known to harbor insurgents attacking traffic on the road. The insurgents fled before the Marines arrived. When the Taliban tried to return several days later, the village leadership fought them off. The villagers were no longer afraid after seeing how quickly the insurgents were defeated at the hands of the Marines.

From the day the Marines arrived, they executed a deliberate campaign plan developed by the platoon commander to influence the area. The platoon made two to three foot patrols each day to nearby villages, as well as one mounted patrol to an outlying village. After several weeks of continuous patrolling and relationship building, the townspeople—especially the shopkeepers and teachers—began cooperating with the troops. During their patrols, the Marines noticed that people appeared supportive or at least indifferent in some villages, while in other areas the population was openly hostile.

The platoon commander insisted that every patrol have a specific mission other than just presence, whether it be to speak with a local shopkeeper, hold a small shura, or gather specific information about the area. The Marines learned to come to every meeting with an agenda but to be patient and engage in casual conversation first. It was not part of local Afghan culture to get to the point quickly. In every meeting, the Marines repeated the same message: they were there to provide security, train the police, and stop anyone who threatened the villagers or Marines.

The Americans demonstrated understanding and compassion without displaying timidity or weakness. They engaged and pursued anyone who shot at them on patrol and never hesitated to dismount and close with the enemy when it made tactical sense. They were ready to engage the population or the enemy as the situation required.

In early July, over 100 insurgents armed with rockets and other heavy weapons attacked the platoon's outpost at the district center. Their plan was to overrun the position, and if that failed, force the Marines to call in air strikes on civilian compounds the insurgents were using as firing positions. The fighting raged for over two hours, but the platoon did not call in air strikes. They exercised restraint, and no civilians were harmed. The Taliban lost at least 13 men before they withdrew.

After the attack, the Marines noticed a change in attitude among the people living around the district center. The Marines heard villagers saying that "there is something different about Marines," that they were stronger than the insurgents. People began cooperating with the Marines, telling them about the valley's tribes and political dynamics.

The Marines eventually learned that there were two dominant Noorzai Pashtun clans in the valley: the Jimalzai and the Khojizai. The Jimalzai, many of whom were teachers and businessmen with some education, were more supportive of the U.S. presence. The Taliban enjoyed strong support in many Khojizai villages. The Marines also learned that the district governor was the seniormost leader among the Khojizai and that he had deliberately misled the Marines about his tribal affiliation.

Rolling the Taliban Back and Rebuilding the Police

In July, 75 local men from the Afghan National Police (ANP) returned from the regional training academy in Shouz in Herat Province in the west. Despite their extra training, the police still lacked basic infantry and marksmanship skills, and corruption and drug abuse were rampant. Individual police officers' main source of income was bribes and extortion, and they were not trusted by the population. The platoon struggled to keep the police from using drugs while on duty.

The district police chief was widely known for incompetence, treachery, and vindictiveness. Police officers complained of beatings and rape, and of fears that they might be murdered in their sleep. By mid-July, 10 officers had deserted and another 30 went on leave and never returned. By the end of July, only 21 policemen remained. The Marines later learned that the police chief's plan was to purge the agency of all men not personally loyal to him, then reconstitute the force with his own people.

The police chief, whom the Marines believed was working for the Taliban, tried several times to lead them into areas where they would be vulnerable to attack. The platoon commander tried repeatedly to have him removed, but to no avail, as the chief had been appointed by the district governor, who had connections in Kabul. According to the platoon commander, "We had to keep eyes in the back of our head. All we could do was mitigate his ability to threaten us, by keeping at least two Marines for every one police, in order to keep the police from becoming a liability in a gunfight."

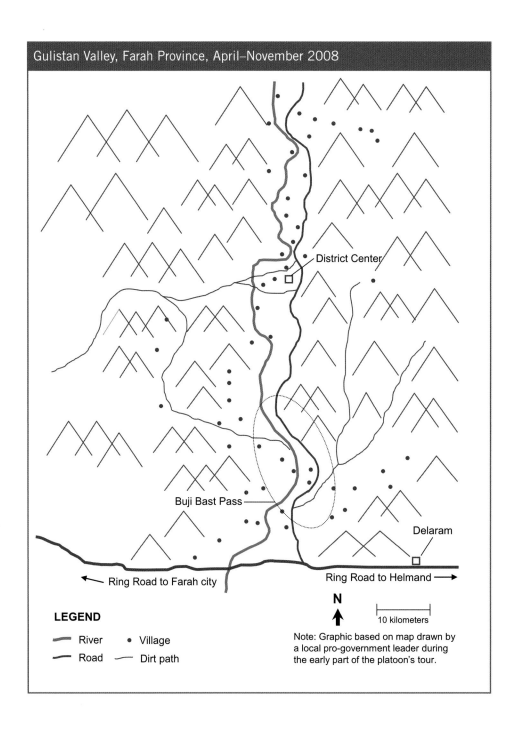

Gulistan Valley, Farah Province, April–November 2008

District Center

Buji Bast Pass

Delaram

Ring Road to Farah city

Ring Road to Helmand

LEGEND

River   • Village

Road   — Dirt path

N

10 kilometers

Note: Graphic based on map drawn by
a local pro-government leader during
the early part of the platoon's tour.

View of the Gulistan Valley.
(Photo by U.S. Marine Corps)

Immediately after the return of the newly minted officers, the Taliban threatened them and kidnapped their relatives. Insurgents kidnapped an engineer from Kabul who was in charge of building a forward operating base for the platoon near the district center. The Taliban also stepped up its campaign of intimidation against the population, including sending night letters to the teachers at the local boys' school as well as to villagers suspected of cooperating with the Marines. The platoon split into three rifle squads and conducted four weeks of continuous patrolling in the district center. The idea was to prevent the insurgents from intimidating the police, so the police could train with them. The insurgents backed off and focused on outlying villages.

In late July, eight kilometers north of the district center, insurgents kidnapped, tortured, and killed three Tajik policemen returning home on leave. The district police chief—who viewed the Tajiks in his force as a threat to his power in the valley—had reportedly told insurgents that the policemen would be traveling that way. When the Marines tried to recover the bodies, insurgents trapped the convoy in a well-laid L-shaped ambush. As the Marines and police moved south toward their base, they were hit again.

In early August, 40 to 50 Taliban ambushed a squad of Marines as it tried to establish a cordon around a village believed to be harboring insurgents. An eight-hour firefight ensued in which the Americans drove the insurgents out of the village. The next day, the village elders came to the district center and held a shura with the platoon commander. The elders expressed gratitude to the Marines for sparing innocent lives in the house-to-house assault through the village and indicated that more than 20 insurgents had been killed.

Despite these engagements, which took a heavy toll on the local Taliban and improved the stature of the Marines, the security situation remained precarious in most of the district's villages. The insurgents continued to control much of the valley. More police deserted in August when the chief let them go "on leave," knowing that they would not come back. By the end of the month, only nine officers remained of the original 75.

The Marines decided that the situation in the police force had become intolerable. They pushed the district governor and police chief to reconstitute the force with local recruits and send them away for training. According to the platoon commander, "They [the district governor and police chief] said, 'we've got this cousin and that cousin, and we will give them a weapon and a uniform.'" The Marines had serious misgivings but believed they had no choice except to leave recruitment to the district government. The police chief got what he wanted—the dissolution of the existing force, which represented various ethnic and tribal groups in the district, and its replacement by a force personally loyal to him and drawn largely from a single clan.

In mid-August, the Marines faced another crisis related to the construction of the forward operating base near the district center. The Kabul-based contractor in charge of the project had not paid the workers in more than two months. People had come from all over the valley to work on the project, many of them farmers who had left their fields uncultivated for the summer. Many of the workers had borrowed against their promised wages, and had fallen into debt with local money-lenders. The workers trusted the Marines, believing they would eventually be paid. By fall, the workers still had not been paid and, although work was nearly complete, most men returned to their fields. The Marines attempted to repay the villagers through various means of barter, such as food and fuel, but the debt was simply too great.

In late August, the Taliban began leaving the district and regrouping in more remote areas to the east. Locals began telling the Marines that the insurgents had left the northern part of the district, though attacks continued around the Buji Bast Pass along the southern edge of the valley. In October, the district governor began cooperating openly with the Marines for the first time.

Reports of Taliban intimidation ceased, and children returned to school. Farther south near the Buji Bast Pass, villagers confronted the Taliban, telling them to leave and never return. In November, many local officials who had been victims of intimidation returned to work in the bazaar and at the forward operating base. They dealt openly with the Marines.

During the last week of November, the Marines turned over command to a platoon from 3d Battalion, 8th Marines. Although there continued to be attacks in the southern part of the valley and reports of insurgent movement on routes between Helmand and Farah, the Taliban was no longer in control in most of the area, and security was much improved. These gains endured through 2009 and into 2010.

Conclusion

The Marines in Gulistan operated on their own in one of the most remote areas of Afghanistan, far from higher headquarters, reinforcements, and re-supply. The platoon had little time to prepare and knew almost nothing about the area going in. The Marines were surrounded by Taliban-controlled territory and forced to work with local officials who were actively collaborating with the enemy.

Such conditions put considerable pressure on the Marines. To operate effectively—perhaps even to survive—they had to be creative, flexible, and aggressive. The platoon commander had to become an expert in area politics, sift through deceitful claims of treacherous officials, identify potential supporters and detractors, and fight off large groups of proficient enemy fighters—all in an environment of persistent Taliban intimidation of the local population. These tasks went far beyond the unit's original mission to simply train the local police.

Dealing with the police proved to be the platoon's greatest challenge. Corruption and drug abuse were rampant, and morale was terrible. Worst of all, the district police chief worked for the Taliban. He systematically abused the men under his command, with the express intention of forcing them to desert. With no way to build a viable police force with such a man at the helm who could not be removed, the Marines had no choice but to work with him.

Despite these obstacles, the Marine platoon managed to push back the Taliban, regain control of the Gulistan Valley, and secure the support of much of the population.

According to the platoon commander, the key to his unit's success was the flexibility to accept and deal with a certain level of corruption and treachery, and above all else, demonstrate superior strength and will. The platoon had considerable autonomy to adapt its tactics and operations to the unique conditions it faced.

The unit succeeded because of its disciplined adherence to basic infantry principles and thorough pre- and post-combat action process. A basic understanding of the concepts of counterinsurgency, coupled with a solid grasp of infantry tactics (with a bias toward speed and maneuver), ensured the platoon's ability to tackle the complexity of tribal networks, while enabling it to prevail in every tactical engagement.

U.S. Marine Battalion
Nawa, Helmand, 2009

In the summer of 2009, 1st Battalion, 5th Marine Regiment (1/5) undertook an operation to clear and hold a Taliban stronghold in the Nawa District of Helmand Province.

In June, 300 Marines joined a small contingent of British and Afghan soldiers already in Nawa to patrol near their base and draw insurgents into the district center. Two weeks later, the remainder of the battalion closed in on the center from the north, south, and west. After two days of fighting, the Taliban was tactically defeated.

The Marines quickly transitioned from combat and clearing operations to stability and holding operations that included befriending locals, holding community shuras, and conducting small reconstruction projects.

Throughout their deployment, the battalion's priority was to provide security for local Afghans. To do so, the Marines spread out into 26 outposts over 400 square miles of farmland and desert. They conducted multiple daily foot patrols along with Afghan National Army (ANA) and Afghan National Police (ANP) forces—collectively known as Afghan National Security Forces (ANSF)—for the primary purpose of talking to locals and creating alliances with key leaders. While locals were initially hesitant to cooperate with the Marines and ANSF, the presence and actions of the Coalition gained the Afghans' trust over time.

While the Marines were managing the security situation, the battalion commander worked closely with the new district government representatives to help promote local governance. He also formed close relationships with the British stabilization advisor,

---

Nawa District is also known more formally as Nawa-I-Barakzayi District, reflecting the dominant Pashtun tribe in the district, the Barakzai.

Unless otherwise noted, information in this vignette comes from interviews with U.S. Marines from 1st Battalion, 5th Marine Regiment on 24 and 25 February; 22, 29, and 30 March; 21, 27, and 28 April; and 6 and 19 May 2010

USAID representative, and civil affairs officer to ensure unity of effort. Together, they held community shuras to discuss major Afghan concerns and visited villages to conduct impromptu shuras with local leaders. Working with key leaders also allowed them to devise a reintegration campaign for villagers who had low levels of involvement with the insurgency.

In addition, the battalion helped Afghans rebuild the district's infrastructure. They cleared canals, built roads, improved small bridges, and opened schools and clinics. Once security was provided, the Coalition arranged projects to win over locals and stimulate the economy using information collected by the Marines during their patrols and shuras. Within weeks of the Marines' arrival, Afghans began to return to Nawa. The district center was transformed from a ghost town to a relatively secure and lively marketplace.

A British Platoon Surrounded

In 2006, a small British Operational Mentor and Liaison Team (OMLT) was sent to Nawa to mentor Afghan soldiers and police. The British and ANSF, collectively known as Task Force Nawa, were outnumbered by Taliban fighters and became pinned down with heavy daily firefights. The British in Nawa lacked the manpower to conduct daily patrols. When they did patrol, they could rarely travel far outside their patrol base at the district center. The task force became tactically isolated and was only accessible by helicopter as Taliban fighters encircled the base. As a result, the British had little access to the population and, in turn, knowledge, about what was happening outside their base. Beyond their small security zone, the Taliban had freedom of movement.

During this time, there was no Afghan government in place. By 2009, the district governor had not been to Nawa in two years. The Taliban taxed, threatened, and stole from locals; closed schools; and generally controlled the area. Many of the locals fled. Only a handful of the approximately 120 shops in the district center's main bazaar remained open.

These conditions prevailed until the summer of 2009 when the U.S. Marines deployed to Southern Afghanistan.

Shaping Operations in Nawa

In the early summer of 2009, the Marines worked with the British military to devise a plan to drive the Taliban out of Nawa. In late June, 300 Marines arrived in the district and joined the British OMLT and ANA soldiers at the district center.

Insurgents attacked the district center as soon as the Marines arrived and continued to attack them every day. For two weeks, the Marines experienced heavy, daily fighting.[1] The Taliban in Nawa were good fighters; they were aggressive and had a basic understanding of infantry tactics. The police fought aggressively and with little restraint—"like cowboys"—alongside the Marines at the schoolhouse. Within days, the Americans began including the ANP on their platoon-sized patrols, expanding the security zone.

The ultimate goal of the U.S. Marine surge in the south was not only to provide security but also to instill confidence in the local population about their government. Shortly after the initial 300 Marines arrived in the district, a new district governor, Haji Abdul Manaf, was appointed to Nawa. Locals knew and respected Governor Manaf from his experience fighting against the Soviets during the 1980s.

Clearing Nawa

In early July, the rest of the battalion entered Nawa as part of a major offensive across Helmand called Operation Kanjar ("Strike of the Sword"). An additional 800 Marines and their ANSF partners conducted movement-to-contact, cleared the district center, and expanded the security zone around the district center.

The Marines encountered little opposition. The Taliban were tactically defeated and relinquished control of the district within 36 hours. While many Taliban fighters were killed, others fled to the nearby town of Marjah or went into hiding.

The battalion dispersed throughout the district into small outposts. Each Marine company was assigned two positions based on the locations of population centers and lines of communication.

The Americans' number one priority was to provide security for the population and, by doing so, to separate the insurgents from the population. They were more concerned with befriending the local populace than hunting down enemy fighters, and they limited the use of mortars and air power.[2] They did not drop a single bomb out of fear of harming civilians and alienating the population. The Marines also reimbursed many locals for damages that occurred during the fighting.[3]

The Marines initially conducted some raids against suspected Taliban leaders; however, after a few missions, they realized that these raids upset the local population while yielding few results. Therefore, these raids were cut back.

Communication with the population was vital to the Marines' success in Nawa. Unlike in other operations, prior to their deployment, the Marines prepared a unified strategic communication plan based on five "enduring talking points" to explain who they were, what was going on, and why they were there. These were as follows:

> 1. We are here in your village/town at the request of your government to help your brave Afghan National Security Forces to make the area safer, more secure, and increase prosperity for the people.

> 2. We are here in partnership with your Afghan security forces. Together, we can improve peace and prosperity in your town.

> 3. We seek your assistance in identifying those who are seeking to destroy your government and keep you in fear. The sooner we can identify these enemies of Afghanistan, the sooner we can remove them from your village.

> 4. Coalition forces have no intention to stay in your village permanently. We will stay long enough to ensure security and will leave when your own security forces can maintain this security on their own.

> 5. We look upon you as our friends. We have left our families to assist you, just as we would for any friend.

Holding Nawa

Before the operation, the battalion expected heavy fighting until September. However, when fighting stopped just two days after their arrival in Nawa, they were forced to transition from combat to stability operations much sooner than anticipated.

The Marines spent the remaining months of their deployment patrolling the area, supporting the expansion of governance, and developing security forces to hold and build the district.

The Marines and ANSF had sufficient numbers to disperse throughout the district. From the initially assigned two company-sized positions, the Marines further dispersed into platoon- and squad-sized outposts, resulting in 26 positions by the end of their deployment. These additional outposts were selected based on areas that the battalion needed to control, such as villages and roads where there had been frequent Taliban activity. Marines at these outposts conducted three to four patrols each day, which reassured locals that Marines were everywhere, providing security. In addition to protecting Afghans, the Americans conducted foot patrols to meet with locals (with the help of interpreters), discover local issues and concerns, and identify local leaders.

At first, however, few locals wanted to talk to the Marines, as the Taliban continued to threaten and intimidate. For example, the Taliban had spread propaganda that the Marines would leave after the August 2009 presidential elections and the Taliban would then regain control of Nawa. Since Nawa had been cleared in the past and the Coalition had never stayed in sufficient numbers to hold the area, local Afghans were inclined to believe the rumors. To demonstrate their lingering presence, the Taliban occasionally left threatening night letters in villages after nightfall to let the population know that they were still around and watching. Villagers also received threatening phone calls. The Marines, however, actively sought to continuously disprove Taliban propaganda—by, for example, staying in the area after elections—and to distinguish themselves from the threatening actions of the Taliban. Marines emphasized the "golden rule": treat others as they would want to be treated if their roles were reversed. They were also apologetic when necessary. The population soon realized that the Taliban could no longer back up their threats, which prompted Afghans to cooperate more freely with the Marines.

The Marines met with locals on every patrol, shaking hands and drinking tea. By doing so, they also differentiated themselves from their British predecessors who had "pointed guns" at locals when they patrolled and had not spent much time talking with them. The Marines were careful to be culturally aware and respectful. For example, they did not enter mosques unless they were invited.

Persistent foot patrolling made the Marines' presence known to the local population. The battalion commander's policy was that no Afghan was to go 72 hours without seeing a Marine or police officer. Some platoons distributed their own version of night letters during night patrols to let people know that the Marines were always around. Many locals began to believe that the Marines never slept.

The Marines used their patrols as an opportunity to collect information about their area. They asked locals about their opinions and top five concerns. Typical questions included

- What changes to the population have there been in the past year? Have people left? Have people returned? Why?

- What are the most important problems? Why?

- Who do you believe can solve your problems? Why?

- What should be done first? Why?

Asking these questions required the Marines to have patience and good "people skills." It was worth the effort, and the Marines familiarized themselves with the area, befriended locals, and prioritized projects.

During their patrols, they also made a conscious effort to identify an area's key leaders and befriend them. After discerning power brokers in their area of operation (AO)—including village elders, tribal leaders, and religious leaders (mullahs)—the Marines met with them at least once a week to drink tea and discuss their concerns. In some cases, these conversations increased in frequency to every other day by the end of their deployment. Many company and platoon commanders took off their gear when talking with elders as a sign of respect. This key leader engagement not only helped the Marines learn more about what the locals needed but also drove operations by providing Marines with more accurate information about who to talk to and what was happening in their area.

The Marines also worked with key leaders on reintegration. From the beginning of their time in Nawa, they advertised that local Afghans who had worked with the Taliban—known to the Marines as the "little t taliban"—should have the opportunity to reintegrate. That is, Marines would forgive past small grievances and not arrest past

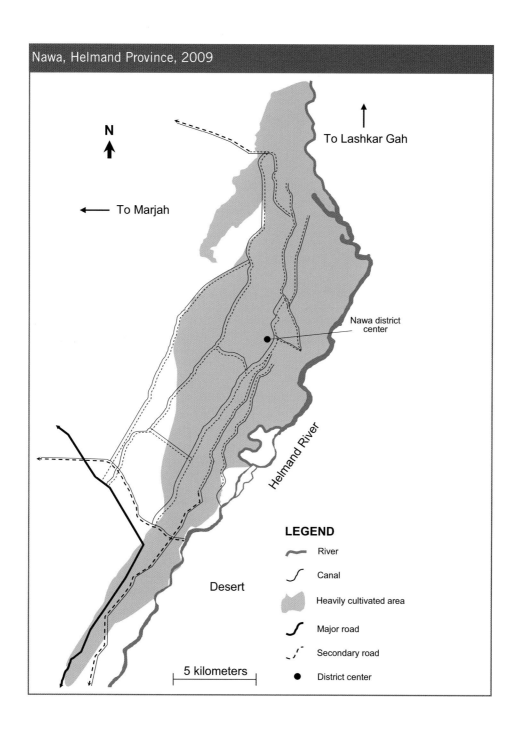

Nawa, Helmand Province, 2009

N

To Lashkar Gah

To Marjah

Nawa district
center

Helmand River

Desert

LEGEND

〜〜 River

∫ Canal

Heavily cultivated area

∫ Major road

‒·‒· Secondary road

● District center

5 kilometers

Platoon commander meeting with locals on a patrol. (Photo by U.S. Marine Corps)

aggressors as long as they were peaceful in the future. By late July, this became an official policy involving the assistance of village elders. In front of their village elders, men pledged not to participate in insurgent actions; by witnessing their pledges, the local elders took responsibility for keeping them straight.

Community meetings, known as shuras, gave the Marines another opportunity to collect information about their respective AO. The battalion commander and district governor walked around to talk with locals in what became known as a "walking shura." Similarly, Marines held impromptu shuras with locals at the platoon and squad levels during their patrols. After discovering ripped-up leaflets in canals, the Marines decided against the routine mass distribution of informational materials. Instead, they began to use the handouts as an icebreaker with which to convene a small impromptu shura. They would have an interpreter on hand to explain the leaflets. The idea was that those Afghans would then take the leaflets back to their village to an educated villager who would read and confirm what they had been told by the Marines. In addition to leaflets, the Marines began to publish a Nawa District newsletter every couple of weeks to explain what was going on in the district. The Marines also relied on policemen to hand out these newsletters in main bazaar areas. Because of low literacy rates, all written products included numerous pictures.

In addition, the Marines distributed radios in a box (RIABs) to locals during their patrols.[4] These radio transmitters had recorded messages from leaders, such as the district governor, police chief, and ANA commander. Separately, the battalion also operated a local radio station and broadcast music, prayers, news, and health messages for the local populace.

The Marines partnered with ANSF at the lowest level of command. They ate, lived, and patrolled side by side with ANP and Afghan National Civil Order Police (ANCOP). They also planned most operations together. On every patrol, the Marines encouraged positive ANP interaction with the populace; for example, they encouraged the police to distribute flyers and to stay to answer questions.

Upon arrival, one Marine likened the ANP to the Mexican Federales because they only behaved when closely monitored. If the Marines did not closely watch them, a policeman might smoke hashish or carry away a farmer's chicken. In October, the local ANP were sent to the police academy as part of the eight-week focused district development (FDD) program. Additional ANCOP were sent to the area to take their place. Although the locals initially preferred them to the ANP, they ended up requesting their local police back because they were more familiar with the area. After the ANP returned from their training, the Marines noticed a slightly more professional force. Their behavior also improved the longer they spent with the Marines. By the end of the 1/5 deployment, some of the ANP even tried to mirror the Marines' appearance by cutting their hair in Marine fashion.

Even when the ANP were not present, the Marines tried to build up police credibility among locals by talking about the positive things the ANP had done. Posters of police officers with Afghans were displayed in bazaars to improve how the locals perceived the ANP and to give the police themselves a constant reminder of professionalism.

A few weeks after the Marines cleared the area, shops began to open and residents began to return to Nawa. Many residents had fled north to Lashkar Gah but returned once they heard through word of mouth that security was improving. By the end of October 2009, the Marines noted that at least 80 of the 120 shops were open in the district center bazaar, demonstrating that locals had growing faith in the economy and the security environment.

By the end of the Marines' deployment, local Afghans had started to take responsibility for their own security. IED incidents decreased by 90 percent.[5]

As security improved, locals approached the Marines about other issues, such as health care and irrigation. Lack of water was always an issue. The Marines listened to the problems but emphasized that the solutions were the district government's responsibility. However, the Marines helped the government by providing funds and equipment for projects. In essence, the Marines served as a broker, which demonstrated to locals that everyone was working together. The Marines also conducted numerous confidence-building projects, including clearing canals and building roads. Each platoon had a budget—almost exclusively funded by the Commander's Emergency Response Program (CERP)—but local village elders decided on projects. Locals were hired to do all the building.

Even though Helmand had the most opium poppy cultivation in Afghanistan, and Nawa District was the second-largest cultivator in the province in 2008, the Marines (unlike their ANSF counterparts) avoided participating in poppy eradication. In conjunction with the Helmand provincial reconstruction team, however, they did help push out wheat seed distribution during the planting season in the fall. They also discussed opium poppy planting with locals and recommended that they not grow it the next season.

Building Nawa

By providing security, the Marines were able to help foster the development of local government. The battalion commander created strong ties to the new district governor and other local leaders and was so widely respected by the population that he became known as "Colonel Bill" throughout the district. The battalion commander and district governor began attending community meetings together to build confidence in the Afghan government, and the district governor and administrator went out in the district center every day and to outlying areas at least twice a week. While the people did not trust the central government in Kabul, they trusted the provincial and district leadership.

The battalion commander was able to work closely with the U.S. and British civilians in the area. Within a month of arriving, the Helmand PRT sent a British stabilization advisor to the district from another part of the province, and the battalion was also assigned a USAID representative. Both civilians, in addition to a civil affairs reservist, worked closely with the battalion commander and his Marines.

At least once a week, the battalion held a high-profile community outreach shura to discuss major district issues and concerns. These shuras typically involved the battalion commander, district governor (and in some cases the provincial governor), district administrator, USAID representative, and British stabilization advisor, therefore demonstrating a united front. Each week these meetings were held in a different part of the district. The first, in late July, involved the provincial governor. Platoons advertised these shuras during their patrols, and more locals attended them as time went on.

These planned shuras allowed the battalion and Afghan government officials to address big issues, such as civilian deaths and Taliban propaganda. For example, early in their deployment, a Marine sniper team killed a farmer who was irrigating at night, mistakenly believing that he was planting an IED. The battalion held a large shura afterward to apologize to locals and admit their mistake.

These shuras also helped address Taliban propaganda. For example, the Taliban spread rumors that the Marines were there to change the Afghan lifestyle. The Marines, however, quickly tried to emphasize that they wanted to help improve the local Afghan lifestyle and provide Afghans with the security necessary to allow for political discussions. Local concerns seemed to be assuaged rather quickly once a commanding officer addressed it at a shura.

Despite improvements in security, there were also setbacks. In late September, the PRT worked with the district government to build a 46-member community council in Nawa (including a handful of known former Taliban). The district governor persuaded elders to reconstitute a traditional council featuring locally selected representatives from each subdistrict. Unfortunately, after the community council was created, insurgents assassinated three of its members, all former Taliban. Their deaths, however, only seemed to strengthen the community council's resolve and reaffirm their belief that they needed

Local Afghan men attend a shura in the Nawa District, Helmand Province. (Photo by SSgt William Greeson, U.S. Marine Corps)

to continue. For security purposes, the council members all stayed in a house together, which forged a bond between them.

As winter approached, the locals became worried because the Marines they knew were about to be replaced by a different Marine battalion.[6] The outgoing Marines eased their fears by introducing their replacements to locals and key leaders and distributing flyers explaining the transition.[7]

Conclusion

During the summer and fall of 2009, the Marines conducted a population-centric counterinsurgency campaign in Nawa. Because they faced far less resistance than expected, they began executing the "hold" aspect of the operation within days of the "clear." The Marines transitioned quickly from a situation that they thought would be heavily kinetic to a heavy civil affairs and information operations (IO) focus to favorably influence local perceptions. They were flexible and quickly adapted to a campaign of "handshakes and smiles."

Throughout their campaign, the battalion's enduring mission was to protect locals from the Taliban threat and win their confidence. The concentration of force, with the recommended troop-to-population ratio, pushed Taliban fighters out and then protected the population by daily foot patrols. Ultimately, the population did not care who provided security, as long as it was provided. While there was some early hesitation to cooperate, locals seemed fed up with being bullied by the Taliban. By living among the people and reassuring Afghans that they would be there for "as long as it takes," the Marines gave villagers a sense of security. The return of families was a sign of progress.

The relatively secure environment allowed the Marines to build personal relationships and trust with locals. The battalion realized that "building castles and wearing heavy armor" would distance them from the people. Therefore, they operated in small units (alongside ANSF) and walked everywhere to focus on befriending the populace, not hunting the Taliban. This required patrols to have tactical patience—to spend time drinking cups of tea and shaking hands with locals—and not rushing to get back to the base. By taking the time to talk with residents and build these relationships, the Marines were able to collect better intelligence that they could use to hunt insurgents.

Understanding the local population was a priority. Squad leaders, platoon leaders, and company commanders were all responsible for analyzing the civilian communities and befriending local leaders in their respective areas of operation. It took some time for Marines to get used to the Afghan schedule and their customs (e.g., irrigating at night), but they learned quickly and were able to adapt to local circumstances.

Information operations was the primary driving force behind all Marine actions and was integrated throughout all activities. As part of their IO campaign, the Marines did not make big promises at the beginning of their deployment and were careful not to promise anything they could not deliver. Even as the end of their tour approached, the outgoing 1/5 Marines distributed informational materials, explained the troop transition, mentored their replacements, and introduced them to locals and key leaders to assuage the people's fears.

After the battalion's focus on security, governance and development followed. The Marines worked to build the credibility of the district government and security forces while maintaining security. The battalion commander created strong ties with capable Afghan and civilian partners, and his company commanders mirrored him. It also helped that all of the company commanders had former counterinsurgency experience in Iraq.

Through large community outreach shuras and small impromptu shuras, the Marines—from the battalion commander to the squad leader—worked with local leaders to identify community problems and gain a better understanding of what was happening in their area. The Marines were outside the wire every day talking with locals and addressing concerns, such as civilian casualties or misperceptions spread by the Taliban. In addition, they helped the local government fund and supply local development projects.

U.S. Marine Advisors
Tagab Valley, Kapisa, 2008

From April to November 2008, a group of U.S. Marine advisors worked with the Afghan National Army (ANA) to clear, hold, and build the southern portion of the Tagab Valley, east of Kabul. The ANA's 201st Corps, 3rd Brigade, had sole responsibility for the area. Afghan soldiers managed to stabilize the valley with minimal Coalition support.

The ANA planned and led the operations in southern Tagab, but Marine advisors were involved at every level of command, from the corps (division) level down to the *kandaks* (small battalions) on the ground. The Marine advisors also pushed for the operations and convinced the ANA that they would succeed.

The southern Tagab Valley was a stronghold of Pakistan-based insurgents responsible for numerous large-scale attacks in eastern Afghanistan. Enemy fighters moved freely through the area and controlled the population. There was no government presence in 2008.

This case is significant because, for the first time, the Afghan army managed to seize ground from the Taliban and hold it with little Coalition assistance. The success of the operations demonstrated that battlespace can be turned over to Afghan units, provided they are ready and have good leadership.

The Struggle Over the Tagab

When the Marines arrived in April 2008, the Tagab Valley was considered a no-go area where insurgents moved freely. Enemy fighters moving into the valley from the east posed a threat to Kabul, Afghanistan's capital city. Rival militias seeking to control the eastern approach to Kabul had fought over the valley constantly during the 1990s civil

---

Unless otherwise noted, information in this vignette comes from interviews with U.S. Marine advisors to the Afghan army's 201st Corps and its subordinate units.

war, when the valley changed hands about 10 times. Its residents had a reputation for cooperating with whichever outside force happened to be stronger at the moment.[1]

The southern part of the Tagab Valley was almost entirely Pashtun. There were no reconstruction projects or functioning government. Poppy farming and timber smuggling were prevalent and insurgent influence was strong. Local warlords provided Pakistan-based insurgent groups with local fighters. The northern part, on the other hand, was mostly Tajik. Tagab had a functioning government and substantial Coalition presence. The district governor was a Tajik distrusted by the Pashtuns to the south.

There had been several operations to clear the southern Tagab in 2005, 2006, and 2007. In 2005, U.S. forces pushed into the valley, forcing the insurgents to flee to nearby valleys and into Pakistan. The soldiers then left, and the insurgents returned as strong as before.[2] In 2006, U.S. forces cleared through the valley a second time and

Afghan soldiers line up to march into the Tagab Valley. (Photo by U.S. Marine Corps)

left Afghan police behind to hold the area. Insurgents overran the police posts in 2006 and again in 2007, after which the police refused to man the positions. In 2007, the Taliban claimed full control over southern Tagab.[3]

The ANA Goes In

In May 2008, Afghan soldiers and police—with U.S. support—launched a large-scale poppy eradication operation in Tagab District. Afghan soldiers moved with the police up the valley, providing security while the police destroyed poppy fields. Barely a shot was fired as about 250 Afghan soldiers and police moved through the valley in four-wheel-drive trucks.

No forces were left behind after the poppy eradication operations. The campaign involved sweeping through the valley, destroying poppy crops, and then leaving. The ANA and their advisors later decided that if they could move through the valley with so little resistance, they might be able to hold it and even begin reconstruction.

The Marine advisors believed that, given past precedent, the police would not be able to hold the valley on their own. The ANA would have to set up permanent bases and patrol the area indefinitely, with the police in a supporting role. The Marines managed to persuade the U.S. military command to give the Afghan army sole responsibility and operational control over southern Tagab.

In June and July, the ANA started moving forces and supplies to the southern mouth of the valley. The plan was to move from there into the southern part of the valley, set up a forward operating base, and push farther north, setting up patrol bases at the mouths of smaller valleys leading into the southern Tagab. At the same time, another group of ANA soldiers and their trainers pushed south from the Tajik areas in northern Tagab.

A U.S. Marine trainer and his interpreter talk with villagers in the Tagab Valley. (Photo by U.S. Marine Corps)

In September 2008, ANA engineers improved the road to the southern mouth of the valley and built a bridge over the Naghlu River. They then began pushing slowly into the valley itself, improving the road as they went. Their intention was to eventually pave the road through the valley, opening up a shorter route between Pakistan and Central Asia that would bypass the treacherous Jalalabad Pass.

Southern Tagab Valley, Kapisa Province, 2008

LEGEND
— River
— Road
■ Lake

To the Panjshir Valley and northern Afghanistan

N

To northern Tagab

Side valleys

Southern Tagab

Naghlu Dam

Sarobi

Jalalabad Pass

Highway to Jalalabad and the Khyber Pass

10 kilometers

Kabul

Ring Road to Kandahar

The ANA engaged with the villages along the river, built patrol bases, and began small-scale reconstruction projects. Despite occasional harassing attacks by the insurgents, most of whom were hiding in smaller side valleys, the Afghan soldiers did not go after them. The ANA built a forward operating base in the southern part of the valley and smaller checkpoints along the valley floor.

The focus was not on clearing the area, but on establishing bases, securing the road, engaging with the population, and beginning reconstruction. It was common knowledge that insurgents operated in significant numbers in the side valleys; however, as long as violence remained low, the ANA and their advisors were willing to leave the insurgents alone. Some of those working for the insurgents were related to local leaders cooperating with the ANA. Afghan army officers and their advisors believed that if they built enough support, those working for the enemy would eventually switch sides.

The Afghan soldiers held shuras in each major village along the river. The ANA brought trucks full of food, clothes, and other supplies to distribute as they went, and Afghan dentists and medics provided some basic medical care. As they moved farther into the valley, they gained momentum: the shuras got bigger and the population, more welcoming.

The ANA led the shuras—the Marine advisors did not speak. Each Afghan army kandak had a religious affairs officer who was a trained *mullah* (a teacher of the Holy Koran), and these men doubled as political officers and did most of the talking. They told villagers that poppy growing was not allowed in Islam and promised the people reconstruction projects in exchange for cooperation.

The ANA, with the Marines' help, executed many reconstruction projects in southern Tagab, especially well construction and medical missions. They also helped the valley's people export pomegranates and saffron to increase profits for the local farmers who had no access to cold storage and had to sell their fruits immediately. Most of the fruit went to Pakistan, where it was stored in refrigerated containers, then exported back into Afghanistan at a 300 percent markup. Subsequently, people from villages farther afield began coming down to the ANA bases and asking for similar projects. Some asked the Afghan army to put patrol bases near their villages.

In October, Afghan soldiers pushed patrols into some of the side valleys where insurgents were operating in greater strength than in the main valley. By November, the main insurgent group in the Tagab began pulling out of the valley, apparently believing that it had lost the support of the population.

Conclusion

The United States can learn important lessons from the operations in the Tagab Valley, including how U.S. forces might eventually transition battlespace to Afghan units. Even after combat forces withdraw, there will still be a need for advisors at multiple levels of command, including on the ground with the kandaks. U.S. Marine advisors have developed a model for readying units for independent operations and transitioning battlespace to Afghan control. For the Marines, the entire purpose of the operations in the Tagab was to transition the battlespace to Afghan control, with as little Coalition support as possible.

The idea was to give the ANA responsibility over a discreet battlespace where no strong U.S. or NATO units overshadowed the Afghan army, and to hold the ANA accountable for what happened there. If the ANA succeeded in southern Tagab, there would hopefully be greater impetus elsewhere to hand over control to the Afghan army. As far as the advisors knew, no strategic plan existed in 2008 to transition battlespace anywhere in the country to Afghan control. It was not a priority for the command in Afghanistan, where the focus was on fighting the insurgency with U.S. and NATO forces.

The success of the operation was due to many factors, among them strong leadership at the brigade and kandak levels, effective Marine advisors at each level of command, the absence of other U.S. or NATO combat units, and the fact that the Afghan army owned the battlespace. The ANA was on its own; it was forced to either operate independently or fail.

When working with the Afghan army, the tendency among most U.S. and NATO forces was to engage in partnering. In practice, this usually meant U.S. units planned and led the operations, with Afghan forces in a subordinate, supporting role. Partnering, which gave little responsibility or latitude to the ANA, often created undue dependency on foreign forces and stifled the ANA leadership, discouraging them from taking the initiative

Afghan army officers lead a shura in a village in the Southern Tagab.
(Photo by U.S. Marine Corps)

or assuming responsibility. This was especially true among more developed Afghan army units that had the capability to operate independently but rarely did so.

According to several advisors, many U.S. and NATO forces operated with the attitude that they owned the area under their control. Those forces did not trust the ANA and shut them out of the planning process. Often, they used Afghan units to achieve tactical objectives without any consideration for the long-term development of the force.

In the Tagab, U.S. Marine advisors did not merely partner with Afghan soldiers for operations and return to their base for the night. The Marines were embedded advisors who lived and worked with Afghan officers and accompanied them on every patrol. The

Marines believed they were particularly well suited to train Afghan soldiers as light infantry, due in part to the Marine culture of "every Marine a rifleman."

The advisors' role was completely different from the roles of other U.S. and NATO forces. The advisors' mission was to ensure that the ANA was used in a way that developed its capability to operate independently. The advisors also provided resources not available to the ANA and backup if needed. These included quick-reaction forces, artillery and air support, and casualty evacuation.

The Marines quickly learned that the ANA's weaknesses were in organization, planning, and logistics. The ANA rarely had the resources to sustain itself in long operations—they needed substantial logistical support. There were also problems with retention, due to long deployments away from home, low pay, and poor working conditions. Individual Afghan soldiers, however, were of high caliber and operated well in small units, especially when they had good leaders.

U.S. Army Battalion
Kunar and Nuristan, 2007–2008

From May 2007 to July 2008, officers of the 1st Squadron, 91st Cavalry Regiment (1-91)—also known as Task Force (TF) Saber—immersed themselves in the complex political environment of northeast Afghanistan. Through countless conversations with local people, the battalion gathered information on the area's many tribal and ethnic groups—their viewpoints, interests, and histories of conflict—and used this knowledge to achieve its objectives while significantly reducing levels of violence.

The officers of Task Force Saber preferred to negotiate—rather than simply fight—their way into remote and dangerous areas. They combined political, economic, and military tools to acquire leverage in these negotiations. They built relationships with local leaders, integrated local shuras with the Afghan government, used reconstruction funds to secure support and create incentives for stability, and used military operations to keep the insurgents off balance. The battalion empowered cooperative local leaders and held them responsible for what happened in their areas, while marginalizing the insurgents.

As a result of these efforts, many insurgents stopped fighting; others changed sides as pro-government leaders gained strength. Levels of violence dropped dramatically. Despite these successes, the gains made were not irreversible—much depended on tenuous relationships between local communities and U.S. and Afghan forces. Maintaining

---

Unless otherwise noted, information in this vignette comes from interviews with 1-91 officers at Forward Operating Base Naray in early March 2008, including the battalion commander, his nonkinetic effects officer, headquarters troop commander, civil affairs officers, information operations officers, and border police trainers. The author also interviewed several local journalists working on the base, and attended shuras with leaders from Ghaziabad District in Kunar and Kamdesh in Nuristan. This vignette also draws on an article by Nathan Springer titled "Implementing a Population-Centric Counterinsurgency Strategy, Northeast Afghanistan, May 07– July 08," *Small Wars Journal* 6 (2010): 1–19, http://smallwarsjournal.com/blog/2010/03/implementing-a-populationcentr/.

these relationships required constant effort. Continuous patrols and engagement in the communities was essential to build relationships, gain local understanding, and sustain support and coordination.

The battalion's area of operations included northern Kunar and eastern Nuristan—some of the most remote and inaccessible terrain in Afghanistan. The people lived in a series of isolated river valleys separated by ridgelines as high as 14,000 feet. Each valley was like a separate country, its people suspicious of outsiders and often armed to the teeth. Nuristan was one of the last areas to be conquered by Afghan rulers and converted to Islam. The Soviet army in the 1980s faced some of its most crushing defeats there. It was also one of the most dangerous for U.S. forces.

Navigating the Political Terrain

The soldiers of 1-91 arrived in Afghanistan in May 2007 intent on pursuing a population-centric strategy. The battalion commander, a former history professor at West Point, was a student of counterinsurgency. His plan was to focus on local engagement and building relationships, targeted use of reconstruction funds, organization of local shuras, and political negotiation.

Understanding what might motivate a community to turn against the insurgency required an in-depth understanding of the area and its politics. The officers of Task Force Saber spent the early part of their tour talking to as many local people as they could—learning about local politics, tribes, economics, and cultural traditions. The soldiers sat with villagers for hours at a time, day in and day out, just to put together a basic picture of the area's complex political dynamic.

In the district of Ghaziabad in northern Kunar, also part of 1-91's area of operations (see map), there were five main groups: the Mushwanis, Salarzais, Gujjars, Kohistanis, and Nuristanis. Mushwanis and Salarzais are Pashtuns, while Gujjars, Kohistanis, and Nuristanis are separate ethnic groups that speak different languages. There were also semi-nomadic groups from Chitral in Pakistan who crossed into Kunar and Nuristan during the winter when the passes in Pakistan were blocked by snow.

These groups did not get along. The Nuristanis of Ghaziabad, whose villages were deep in the mountains away from the Kunar River, refused to accept or participate in any

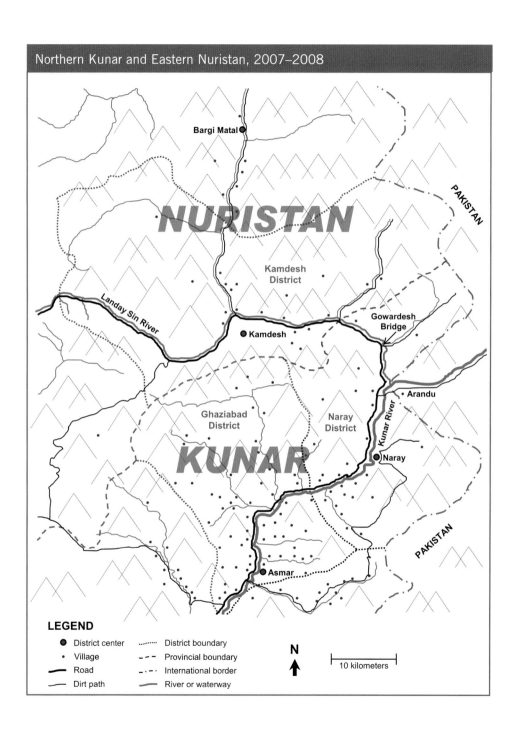

Northern Kunar and Eastern Nuristan, 2007–2008

PAKISTAN

Bargi Matal

NURISTAN

Kamdesh
District

Landay Sin River

Kamdesh

Gowardesh
Bridge

Arandu

Ghaziabad
District

Naray
District

Kunar River

KUNAR

Naray

Asmar

PAKISTAN

LEGEND

● District center .... District boundary
• Village – – – Provincial boundary
▬ Road –·–· International border
— Dirt path ▬ River or waterway

N

10 kilometers

shuras with the Pashtun tribes and did not recognize the Pashtun-dominated district and provincial governments. Gujjar leaders had allied with the Russians during the Soviet occupation in the 1980s and were considered persona non grata by Pashtuns, Kohistanis, and Nuristanis alike. There were also divisions within these communities that were not so easy to discern. They fought among themselves constantly.

Beyond the ethnic dimensions, there were numerous disputes between various villages and clans, particularly in Ghaziabad District. Many of these were over land, access to water, and money. Projects that ran through or affected several villages—such as roads, pipe schemes, or micro-hydro projects that promised to deliver electricity to multiple villages—often led to serious conflicts that jeopardized these projects. Outside contractors—basically, anyone not part of the local community—were viewed as a threat. The district government was ineffective when it came to resolving these problems. There was also constant fighting between armed groups over control of natural resources, especially timber and gems smuggled into Pakistan.

The fighting in Nuristan was wrapped up in the politics of the region and had little to do with religious radicalism or al-Qaeda and the Taliban. In some cases, bitter rivalries between local power brokers led one side to join the government and the other, the insurgents. Coalition raids based on misinformation—often deliberately false information passed to U.S. forces by local power brokers looking for creative ways to eliminate their enemies—had pushed many toward the insurgents during earlier years of the war.

The battalion, which acquired a reputation as an honest broker through repeated meetings with local leaders and the building of relationships based on trust, refused to take sides in local disputes for fear of getting drawn into local feuds. The soldiers of 1-91 built consensus through frequent dialogue and enabled community shuras to resolve disputes.

Task Force Saber also used these shuras to improve security. For example, in July 2007, the battalion reached out to the Nuristanis of Ghaziabad District. The commander realized that the Nuristanis had been marginalized in the district government and that U.S. forces were basically at war with them. After a major attack on a U.S. convoy attributed to Nuristani militants in Ghaziabad, a group of Nuristani elders came to the battalion headquarters at Forward Operating Base (FOB) Naray. They agreed to put pressure on the militants to stop the attacks in exchange for political recognition and reconstruction projects. Illegal checkpoints and attacks on convoys in Ghaziabad decreased dramatically thereafter.

In August 2007, the battalion reached out to the leaders of an openly hostile village eight kilometers south of Naray. The village of Saw had been the site of a botched nighttime raid in the winter of 2005—a cause of dishonor for which the village sought revenge by launching frequent rocket attacks. It was considered a no-go area when 1-91 arrived.

From August to November 2007, TF Saber began visiting the village regularly and meeting with its leaders. The battalion also sent school supplies. The next day, village leaders delivered 100 thank you notes written in Pashtu by the village's children. As the relationship grew, 1-91 began construction of a clinic, a school, and a bridge. U.S. and Afghan soldiers visited the village regularly to discuss the projects and to provide medical assistance. The village leaders gradually halted insurgent movement through their lands.

In early 2008, the battalion built a bridge in Saw that crossed the Kunar River— the only bridge for miles around. Men from the village guarded the bridge around the clock and repulsed several attacks on the project. By the end of its tour, TF Saber had managed to secure the cooperation of 40 villages that were earlier considered hostile. Some of these villages raised their own self-defense forces to protect their communities. These villages had become invested in the reconstruction that the battalion was providing and were keen to protect these projects.

In the summer of 2007, the battalion reached out to elders in the dangerous and nearly inaccessible district of Kamdesh in Nuristan. That summer, there were several large firefights in Kamdesh, as well as many small-scale attacks. By October, elders began an organized effort to pressure the insurgents to stop fighting. In early 2008, the soldiers helped put together a shura of 100 local leaders representing different villages. These leaders traveled around the district trying to persuade people to stop supporting the insurgency and engage with the government.

The elders met frequently with TF Saber officers and sometimes accompanied them on patrol as a show of support. The battalion commander traveled to Kamdesh to meet them as well. In March 2008, the elders traveled to FOB Naray—a long and dangerous journey—and met with the 1-91 battalion commander. They then traveled to Kabul, met with President Karzai, and asked him for support.

When insurgents solicited outside support for a major attack in June 2008, local leaders informed Afghan and U.S. forces. As a result, 1-91 was able to defeat a force of 150 or more fighters, dealing a serious blow to the insurgency.

Task Force Saber officers reached out to religious leaders and provided funds to refurbish mosques. Many local mullahs, or religious leaders, had preached against the Coalition and called on local youth to attack U.S. and Afghan forces. They insisted that U.S. soldiers were not to be trusted, that they would burn villages like the Russians had during the 1980s. Some mullahs turned around completely as a result of the battalion's outreach efforts, and began speaking in favor of the Coalition.

A meeting of the Kamdesh shura in Nuristan, March 2008. (Photo by U.S. Army)

The battalion also funded a newspaper and the area's only radio station. A local teacher ran the radio station, which broadcast programs on Islam, local news, and music from India, Pakistan, and Iran. People in far-flung villages sent letters requesting songs. There were programs in different local languages, such as Nuristani, Pashtu, Khoistani, and Gujjari. The battalion fielded thousands of requests for hand-held radios.

Over time, Task Force Saber built a solid base of support in some of the most remote and dangerous areas of Afghanistan, while taking relatively few casualties and causing little harm to civilian life and property. With so few forces and such difficult terrain, the battalion—if it was to be effective and not make enemies needlessly—had little choice but to rely on the population to protect its troops and achieve its objectives.

Using Money to Acquire Leverage

Task Force Saber used its reconstruction funds as part of a targeted effort to build on and strengthen relationships with local communities. The battalion also used funds to empower receptive leaders in key villages. The officers of 1-91 provided funds directly to local leaders and gave them control over projects in their villages, rather than work through outside contractors.

The soldiers did this only after visiting these communities and developing relationships with their leaders. They did not simply contract out projects from the safety of their forward operating base.

The mission of 1-91 was to open up new areas in northern Kunar and eastern Nuristan. Pushing money into these areas was a way to generate popular support and acquire leverage with local leaders, rather than simply rely on combat operations and patrols. According to TF Saber officers, the tactic made soldiers safer by reducing attacks on convoys and patrols.

There was always a quid pro quo—that is, the battalion ensured that it got something in return for its money, whether intelligence or a reduction in attacks. The focus was on gaining and maintaining leverage. The battalion created relationships with key leaders by providing them with reconstruction funds and used the promise of future funds to ensure their continued cooperation. The battalion also used its funds to force quarreling tribes to settle their differences. Feuding clans often came to a consensus quickly, if failing to do so meant getting no money at all. In more remote areas of Nuristan, village leaders sometimes came to the battalion's combat outposts. The soldiers in these outposts negotiated with the elders by asking for information, political support, or security for their patrols in exchange for reconstruction funds.

The battalion also cut off funds as a way to punish village leaders who failed to deliver. For example, in Ghaziabad District, the battalion stopped all reconstruction funds for a month following a series of attacks on supply trucks. The Ghaziabad shura promised to stop the attacks in exchange for a resumption in funding. According to the battalion commander, "cutting off their funding was a more effective stick than going into a village and detaining a bunch of people."

Working with elders to hire engineers, scope projects, and submit proposals gave village leaders a sense of ownership over reconstruction projects. Once the project was approved and some initial funds were available, the unit was then able to apply leverage. For example, 1-91 could then tell village leaders that unless insurgent attacks stopped, they would not see the rest of the funds. This tactic became increasingly effective as time went by.

The leaders of 1-91 learned that simply going after the insurgents without taking the time to build relationships and credibility tended to do more harm than good. Many insurgents in the region were related to people in the villages, including village leaders. Civilian casualties fueled demands for vengeance, even among people not inclined to join the insurgency. Combat operations carried fewer risks and had more lasting effects in communities where the population had turned against the insurgents and isolated them.

Task Force Saber arrived at the conclusion that many local men involved in attacks on U.S. troops were not irreconcilable. Those who fired on U.S. soldiers were not necessarily extremists, much less linked to al-Qaeda. Armed resistance against outsiders—any outsider whether American, Russian, or Afghan—has a long and proud history in northeast Afghanistan.

The battalion's aim was to empower cooperative village leaders, to give them the resources to take charge of their areas, influence their youth, and keep the insurgents out. The battalion did this, at least in part, by giving these leaders control over reconstruction funds spent in their villages—what projects went where and who to hire.

This tactic was a way to counter Pakistani-based insurgent facilitators who paid handsomely for new recruits. Local men were going to Pakistan and returning with money, weapons, and training—upsetting the balance of power in the region. Many set up illegal checkpoints and used their weapons to raid villages in neighboring valleys.

The officers of 1-91 were aware that some of the money given to village elders would be stolen and that some projects could not be adequately monitored. In order to mitigate these problems, the battalion worked to secure community "buy in" for projects by giving them some sense of power and ownership over the construction process and by persuading local leaders to invest their reputations in the successful execution of projects in their villages. Once a group of leaders had set priorities and invested effort to get a project drafted and approved and under local management, their honor was on the line.

In general, projects owned by the local community were done faster, to a higher standard, and with fewer security problems than those contracted to outsiders. When an entire community knew the cost of a project and how many people were supposed to be employed, social pressure against corruption increased. The same process worked for humanitarian assistance.

Combat Operations

Task Force Saber used political negotiation to achieve its objectives, while reducing violence against U.S. and Afghan forces. Local engagement often preceded combat operations and was often the key factor shaping the timing of these operations.

The battalion's combat operations focused on targeting insurgents, interdicting their movement over the border with Pakistan, and protecting its forward positions. These missions required the battalion to expand its influence into the remote areas of Kunar and Nuristan.

The geography of northern Kunar and Nuristan is extremely restrictive—dominated by high mountains and isolated valleys, many of them accessible only by air. The battalion was able to safely secure only the populations along the Kunar River. There were plenty of places beyond the Coalition's reach where insurgents could take refuge. The terrain was too difficult and the area too large to dominate through sheer force presence.

Until the summer of 2008, the soldiers could not drive more than 10 kilometers north of their main base without being attacked. The most serious attacks on convoys occurred in Nuristan during the summer of 2007. Some large-scale ambushes involved 50 to 100 insurgents. Nuristani insurgents operated numerous illegal checkpoints. They also hit trucks in Ghaziabad District. The soldiers at FOB Naray spent considerable time trying to stop these attacks.

Though there were many attacks on the roads—most of them in 2007—it was extremely rare for 1-91 soldiers to come under fire in or near a village. This was particularly true in villages that the battalion had engaged with in the past. Village elders sometimes escorted 1-91 troops from one village to the next or between their village and one of the combat outposts. Insurgents never opened fire on a patrol accompanied by local leaders. As the battalion made friends in the villages, it was also able to gather better information about the insurgents, which made kill-capture missions more precise and less likely to harm innocent people or their property.

The insurgents in 1-91's area were well organized, well trained, and heavily armed—particularly in 2007. Each local commander led a gang of young men from his valley, with the help of money, weapons, and training from insurgent facilitators based across the

A U.S. soldier looking over the Gowardesh Bridge in Nuristan in May 2008. (Photo by SSgt Tyffani L. Davis, U.S. Army)

border in Pakistan. For large operations, these facilitators united several local gangs temporarily and gave them extra weapons and money and a plan of attack. Once the operation was over, local fighters dispersed and returned to their villages. Local gangs often fought over illegal checkpoints and control over the region's illicit timber and gem trade.

In April and May of 2008, the battalion launched a major operation to re-establish a strategically located border police checkpoint at a place known as the Gowardesh Bridge in Nuristan. Insurgents had overrun a small police garrison at the bridge in August 2007 after the border police abandoned the position.[1] Task Force Saber officers met with elders from the area to secure their support for the operation. These elders, many of them upset by the numerous illegal checkpoints on the road, asked the insurgents to support the operation or leave. When the troops arrived at the bridge, a group of Nuristani elders came out to greet them. Not a shot was fired.

Conclusion

For the officers of Task Force Saber, understanding local politics was essential to achieving the battalion's objectives without unnecessary fighting. Doing so was not easy. It required earning the trust and support of local leaders through relationship building, constant engagement, and savvy use of reconstruction funds. Most of all, it required patience and a willingness to listen.

TF Saber's effort was more diplomatic than military. Personal relationships underpinned everything the battalion did. Soldiers in outposts provided the security necessary to do what was really important—reach out to the population and negotiate with its leaders, while remaining impartial and staying out of local feuds. It was a population-centric strategy.

In meetings with village leaders, 1-91 officers spent considerable time talking about matters other than the insurgency, such as the harvest, local history, or the weather. It was not part of the culture to get to the point quickly. It took time to build rapport and to get people who were deeply suspicious of outsiders to provide information about the politics of their area. The soldiers of TF Saber engaged with people in their villages, not on the base. They used reconstruction funds to build relationships, empower cooperative leaders, and persuade communities to work with the Coalition.

Task Force Saber's strategy was to move slowly, using relationships, shuras, money, and targeted security operations to influence people and change the local dynamic. The idea was not to throw an entire battalion of soldiers into Nuristan, get into a lot of firefights, and clear the area. The people in northern Kunar and Nuristan were extremely suspicious of anyone not from their particular valley and had a long history of fighting outsiders. The area was too large and the terrain too difficult to clear entirely of enemy fighters. The only alternative was to mobilize the population and turn young men away from the insurgency.

The battalion followed a "do no harm" approach that involved considerable restraint in the use of force. The officers of 1-91 understood that if innocent civilians were harmed—or even local fighters whose friends and relatives resented the killing of their loved ones no matter what their allegiances may have been—the situation could quickly spiral out of control. According to the Task Force Saber commander, "You can't simply kill your way out of an insurgency. The supply of fighters here is inexhaustible."

The battalion commander believed that if he did not move cautiously into Nuristan, it could become like the Korangal—a reclusive valley in central Kunar known for its violent resistance to outside influence. Coalition forces had pushed into the Korangal against the wishes of its leadership, got into firefights, made enemies, and took many casualties.

Vignette 5

U.S. Army Battalion
Khost, 2004–2008

From 2004 to 2008, Khost was one of Afghanistan's most dangerous provinces.[1] Located in eastern Afghanistan, it shares a 112-mile mountainous border with Pakistan's tribal areas. Insurgents from the Haqqani network—the same group that besieged Soviet bases during the 1980s and operated terrorist training camps in Khost during the 1990s—passed back and forth across the border with ease.[2] During the early years of the war, U.S. troops focused on targeting insurgent leaders through raids and cordon-and-search operations, which caused resentment among the locals and undermined the counterinsurgency effort.

In 2007, a U.S. Army battalion and provincial reconstruction team (PRT) in the province began to turn the situation around. Soldiers left their headquarters and dispersed into the province's districts to secure areas and mentor officials. Unlike their predecessors, the battalion spent less time driving in armored convoys and more time among the people. At the same time, the PRT carried out a large number of projects implemented through the Afghan government. These parallel counterinsurgency and development efforts conducted by the maneuver battalion and PRT began to show notable progress, which was amplified by American media.[3] By the end of 2007, the Afghan president and U.S. defense secretary called Khost a model of successful counterinsurgency.[4]

Khost Province is also often spelled "Khowst."

Unless otherwise noted, this vignette is based on interviews and email correspondence with the Khost PRT commander (March 2007–March 2008) on 13 November 2009; Khost PRT commander (March–November 2008) on 21 and 26 January 2010; Khost PRT commander (November 2008–July 2009) on 12 November 2009; PRT Department of State representative (April 2007–August 2008) on 17 July 2010; maneuver battalion commander of 321st Regiment, 82nd Airborne Division (2007–2008) on 13 January 2010; maneuver battalion commander of 4th Battalion, 320th Field Artillery Regiment (February 2008–March 2009) on 20 January, 10 March, and 16 July 2010; company commander in Khost (February–September 2008), 320th Field Artillery Regiment, 101st Airborne Division, on 24 February 2010; and information operations officer for the PRT in Khost (March–November 2008) on 25 February 2010.

In 2008, however, security conditions in the province again deteriorated as the insurgents adapted, new U.S. units rotated in, and conditions changed in nearby Pakistan.

Early PRT Involvement

In 2004, the United States sent its first PRT to Khost, based at Forward Operating Base (FOB) Chapman. From 2004 to 2006, the Khost PRT started reconstruction projects, such as roads and schools, yet progress was minimal. Several commanders were transferred, and the PRT and the province's maneuver battalion did not work together on their development and reconstruction efforts.[5]

In 2006, the PRT began to work more closely with local officials. It participated in district and provincial shuras, and civil affairs teams moved into some district centers to learn about local needs.[6] The PRT began choosing projects through an open bidding process that involved government officials. Cooperation between the PRT and maneuver battalion also improved. For example, the battalion gave the PRT its Commander's Emergency Response Program (CERP) funds for reconstruction to improve unity of effort and streamline decision making.[7]

In August 2006, a new governor, Arsala Jamal, took charge in Khost. Governor Jamal spoke fluent English, had experience working with nongovernmental organizations (NGOs), and was trusted by the Coalition and a significant number of locals. Communication can be a barrier in many areas of Afghanistan, and the fact that Governor Jamal spoke fluent English eased coordination with the Coalition.

Yet despite these developments, Khost became increasingly violent. In the fall of 2006, the Pakistani army pulled out of North Waziristan, the tribal area on the Pakistani side of the border.[8] The Haqqani network, referred to as "the most dangerous and challenging foe for the Coalition forces" in the area, had more freedom to move across the border to Afghanistan as the Pakistani army withdrew.[9] Violence increased and the number of suicide attacks began to rise. By the end of 2006, Khost had more improvised explosive devices (IEDs) than anywhere else in Afghanistan, most of them in Sabari District.

Khost's PRT commander and provincial governor speak at a public event on 16 May 2007. (Photo by PFC Micah E. Clare, U.S. Army)

Fragile Gains: 2007

In Khost, the PRT and maneuver battalion operated from different bases. It took considerable time to move soldiers anywhere within the province. Not only did this hinder their response time to protect the population from enemy activity, but regular road convoys also made the soldiers more vulnerable to IEDs.

In early 2007, the maneuver battalion launched a new campaign. It built three concentric rings of security around the provincial capital, with the Afghan National Police (ANP) and Afghan National Army (ANA) at the two inner rings and the Americans on the outer ring.[10] The general idea was that if the people in Khost City (the provincial capital) felt secure, other aspects of the Coalition's counterinsurgency strategy—such as local governance and reconstruction—would follow.

As a part of this new strategy, much of the battalion moved off the main base and into small patrol bases adjacent to several key district centers that housed the district governor, chief of police, and the town's security forces.

The primary mission for troops at these outposts was to increase security and local governance. Soldiers patrolled with the ANA and ANP almost every day around the district centers. They spent more time engaging with the population than moving in armored convoys. By co-locating and working with officials, U.S. troops were able to build relationships and learn about conditions in each district. Their presence provided "an immediate promise of security, and for the first time, a taste of the rewards of having a government."[11]

In March 2007, the PRT received additional funds, which it used to launch a large number of projects that it coordinated closely with the efforts of the maneuver battalion.[12] Khost received more assistance in 2007 than it had in the previous five years combined, most of it for road projects. In one year, the PRT began to build 300 wells, 50 schools, 6 district centers, 30 irrigation dams, and 50 miles of road, and did not neglect remote areas.[13] These projects, in turn, created local jobs.

The PRT not only increased the number of projects, but also changed the way it managed them. It expanded open bidding for contracts and stopped paying contractors in advance. It also emphasized "getting the story out" on these projects by advertising its activity to the local population so they knew that improvements were being made across the province, as well as highlighting the government's involvement. The PRT included the governor, district governors, line directors, and tribal elders in groundbreaking and grand opening ceremonies. The idea was to show Afghans tangible results of improved security and create a buzz about reconstruction efforts.[14]

During this period, the PRT, the maneuver battalion, and U.S. Army Special Forces (SF) worked more closely together than before and met weekly with the governor to coordinate initiatives and responses to problems. The maneuver battalion commander limited nighttime raids and worked closely with the special forces operating in the area. In earlier years, SF units in the province, which fall under a separate chain of command, had often carried out raids without informing the battalion or PRT—sometimes in villages where conventional forces were trying to build support through nonkinetic activities, thereby undermining the counterinsurgency effort.

Even though there was significant insurgent activity, relations between the Coalition and the local population improved.[15] Security improved in the district centers to the point where the PRT commander felt safe enough to stay the night. The percentage of IEDs turned in by Afghans increased from 30 percent in early 2006 to 60 percent by March 2007.[16] 0Religious leaders also issued religious rulings, known as *fatwas*, condemning suicide bombings.[17] As security improved, NGOs returned. In January 2007, the UN opened an office in Khost for the first time.[18]

Things Fall Apart: 2008

The media coverage of Khost's much-touted success attracted a lot of attention—not only in the United States but also among insurgents. In 2008, the security situation worsened as insurgents went on the offensive to regain control of the province.

In addition, unit rotations in early 2008 halted the Coalition's momentum. Within 30 days, new units replaced the PRT and maneuver battalion, causing the Coalition to lose its local familiarity in the province. At the same time, Governor Jamal left for months to visit his family in Canada. The combination of the unit rotations and an absent strong local partner created a steep learning curve for the new units, especially as they faced an influx of insurgent activity. In March, suicide bombers attacked the district centers in Sabari and Tani within days of each other.

With the turnover of units, the PRT and the maneuver battalion also did not work as closely with the provincial government as they had the year before. After the governor returned from his extended leave, U.S. officers no longer met with him on a daily basis but saw him two to three times a week instead.

Coordination between the maneuver battalion, PRT, and special forces—which had kept night raids to a minimum in 2007[19]—also appeared to break down with the arrival of new commanders and units. The new maneuver battalion and PRT commander did not work as closely together as their predecessors had, and each had different strategies on how to approach the situation. As a result, there was less integration of effort. The previously limited night raids resumed and often special forces conducted raids without informing the battalion or the PRT. Since Afghans do not place much value on the differences between military uniforms, they did not differentiate between the U.S. soldiers they saw daily and the commandoes who raided their homes at night. Locals expressed growing frustration with these night raids.[20]

The new maneuver battalion arrived with fewer forces than the previous unit but was given additional forces as violence grew. In addition to dealing with increased insurgent activity and large insurgent safe havens, the new battalion also gained additional battlespace. More forces were distributed to each outpost for additional force protection. By spring 2008, U.S. troops were positioned alongside the ANA and ANP in at least 7 of the 13 districts. Yet insurgents continued to move freely in many areas during the night, distributing night letters and speaking at mosques.

With additional forces, the new battalion spent more time targeting insurgents and clearing remote areas, in part because of stepped-up enemy activity. In an effort to gain more control, the battalion pushed into insurgent safe havens in outlying areas. As U.S. troops spent more time pursuing the enemy, interaction with the population in the districts declined. U.S. troop presence was especially thin in the villages beyond the district centers. In addition, many villagers reported having never seen a representative of the Afghan government, and many locals could not identify their district governor.[21]

In addition to its increase in clearing operations, U.S. troop distribution in the province also changed. U.S. troops turned over the defense of two district centers to ANA detachments. The goal was to "transfer as many district centers to Afghan National Security Forces (ANSF) control as possible."[22] While the maneuver battalion redistributed its forces in the province, the PRT also decided to punish the restive district of Sabari by ceasing operations there. Security continued to deteriorate. In addition to increased insurgent activity, neighboring villages and rival tribes often fought over reconstruction projects. By the summer of 2008, "no area of Khost was secure from IEDs anymore, the Taliban was gaining political support, and the people's cooperation with the government was deteriorating."[23]

As troop distributions in the province changed, attacks on district centers increased, as did the overall number of attacks. On 20 November 2008, a suicide car bomb nearly destroyed the Domanda District center in Shomal and its adjacent patrol base along the dangerous Khost-to-Gardez Pass. In December, there was another suicide attack outside the Mandozai District center, which killed 14 schoolchildren. Suicide bombers also attacked the main bases of the PRT and maneuver battalion. The attacks signified to locals that the Coalition was losing. In one poll taken at that time, respondents indicated that their perception of security in Khost had declined.[24] By the end of 2008, almost every district had a security problem.

At the same time, the Coalition lost its local partner who had been actively involved in trying to improve the province. In November 2008, Jamal resigned as governor, likely for his own safety. Insurgents had led an effective assassination campaign against many Khost leaders and had tried to assassinate Governor Jamal at least five times during his term.[25] After Governor Jamal's departure, U.S. forces lacked a strong Afghan local leader to work with. Months passed without filling his vacancy. A new governor was finally appointed in January 2009 but soon lost the trust of the PRT and left office seven months later. The security and governance situation continued to fall apart.

Conclusion

U.S. forces made significant progress in Khost in 2006 and 2007. The "Khost model" demonstrated many effective counterinsurgency practices, such as the dispersal of forces into small patrol bases in population centers, constant patrols with Afghan forces, and close Coalition coordination.

Force presence was key. U.S. forces dispersed into platoon-sized outposts next to key district centers, colocated with the local government and security forces. Operating in small units increased mobility, allowed greater access to the local populace, and allowed for daily patrols with the ANA and ANP.

However, the small patrol bases that allowed U.S. forces to sustain presence among the populace were also more vulnerable. In 2008, insurgents increasingly targeted the district centers. Two outposts were destroyed by suicide bombers.

Personalities and relationships mattered. Close cooperation between the commanders of the PRT, the battalion, and the special forces in 2007 minimized the possibility of these units working at cross-purposes. In addition, Governor Jamal was active and effective. Coordination with Afghan officials helped create the sense among the population that everyone was working toward the same goal. By discussing projects with local leaders at shuras and continuing their involvement in the subsequent open bidding process, the PRT helped empower the Afghan government and increase political participation.

In 2008, insurgents launched a renewed campaign of violence and intimidation. At the same time, unit rotations appear to have hindered the Coalition's progress. The PRT and maneuver battalion left the area within a month of each other, leaving the new units to familiarize themselves with the province during a time when the governor was absent. This left a large gap in local understanding for the new forces to fill. Relationships and trust had to be rebuilt, and there was a steep learning curve. In addition, the new commanders did not work as closely with each other as their predecessors had, and unity of effort suffered as a result. Finally, Governor Jamal's resignation, which caused Khost to lose a strong, committed, and trusted governor, made matters worse.

Unfortunately, the gains made by Coalition forces from 2006 to early 2008 were too fragile. Intensified insurgent attacks in conjunction with unit rotations, less Coalition coordination, the loss of an effective governor, and increased U.S. activity across the border undid much of what had been accomplished. As security declined, the people of Khost began to doubt that the Coalition still had the momentum. Stepped-up raids and clearing operations by the Coalition also contributed to a decline in public support. Ultimately, it was premature to call the operation in Khost a model of successful counterinsurgency after only two years of progress.

U.S. Army Battalion
Nangarhar, 2005–2009

This vignette describes how a U.S. Army battalion, provincial reconstruction team (PRT), and agribusiness development team (ADT) took a backseat role to support a strong provincial governor's plan to eliminate opium poppy cultivation in Nangarhar Province in eastern Afghanistan. Unlike in other areas of Afghanistan, the Afghan government took the lead in Nangarhar while U.S. forces stepped aside to support their efforts through training, mentoring, and funding.

Over the course of one year, Nangarhar Province transformed from being a top opium poppy cultivator to being "poppy free." This accomplishment was made possible due to a benign security situation, a powerful governor, and the Coalition's supporting efforts to empower Afghan National Security Forces (ANSF) and provide viable crop alternatives to farmers.

While the local populace initially supported the Taliban in the 1990s for bringing stability to the area, Nangarharis soon realized that the movement was "far too radical" for them.[1] Because the Taliban lacked strong support, U.S. forces were able to force most of them out of the province within a month after arriving in 2001.

After the Afghan provincial government regained control in 2002, insurgent violence remained relatively low in Nangarhar compared to its neighboring provinces. Roadside bombs remained a threat, and attacks continued along the province's long and open border with Pakistan, which allowed insurgents to attack and then retreat.

Unless otherwise noted, this vignette is based on interviews with Department of State Bureau of International Narcotics and Law Enforcement Affairs officers on 18 and 20 November and 6 December; PRT USAID representative (2004–2006) on 14 January 2010; PRT commander (March–November 2008) on 20 April 2010; and maneuver forces commander (May 2007–July 2008) on 26 April 2010. Also, email correspondence with an Army civil affairs officer at the Nangarhar PRT (June 2005–June 2006) and counternarcotics team member (February 2007–November 2009) on 15 January 2010.

In 2005, a former warlord from southern Afghanistan became governor of Nangarhar. Despite his reputation as a corrupt leader involved with the drug trade in the south, he proactively pursued a ban on opium poppy in Nangarhar in 2007. His persuasive and powerful personality helped convince local tribes to stop growing opium poppy, and he kept district-level government leadership from participating in the drug trade. At the same time, he worked with the Coalition to reward districts for their compliance with the opium ban by awarding development projects and used his own funds to help reconstruct the capital city of Jalalabad.

The relatively stable security situation and strong governor allowed the Coalition in Nangarhar to focus on supporting the provincial government's efforts with development and reconstruction. At first, the Coalition focused on efforts to help stimulate the economy in Jalalabad, once considered the economic hub of eastern Afghanistan.[2] After the province's PRT arrived in 2003, it focused on roads, bridges, irrigation systems, power, health clinics, and schools. Nangarhar became one of the largest recipients of aid in Afghanistan. By 2007, the PRT was focusing many of its projects on leveraging the governor's success in poppy eradication. At the same time, insurgent attacks decreased in Nangarhar even though they increased in neighboring provinces.

Due to Nangarhar's relative security and the general competence of the local government and ANSF, Afghans also took the lead in providing security for the province. U.S. military forces took a supporting role by training Afghan National Police (ANP) and helping to establish a Joint Provincial Coordination Center (JPCC) in 2008 to coordinate actions between the ANSF and Coalition.

A Strong Governor

In June 2005, the Coalition gained a strong local partner when Gul Agha Sherzai was appointed governor of Nangarhar. A Barakzai Pashtun from Kandahar, Sherzai fought with the *mujahideen* against the Soviets and had a history of opposing the Taliban. He was the governor of Kandahar from 1992 until 1994, when the Taliban forced him into exile.

In 2001, with the help of U.S. forces and his own personal militia, Sherzai led a force into Afghanistan to reclaim Kandahar. He was officially reappointed governor of Kandahar in December 2001. After he was appointed, his militia undermined security by taxing and threatening the population; he alienated some tribes by favoring others; and he made an estimated fortune of $300 million through the opium trade and illegal taxes at the Pakistani border.[3] President Karzai removed him from power in August 2003.

Karzai reassigned Sherzai to Nangarhar in 2005, when it was considered one of the most troublesome areas in the country, primarily due to its high level of opium poppy cultivation. Governor Sherzai did not have any tribal connections in Nangarhar and quickly learned that he would need to alter his behavior to maintain influence. He began to build a network of supporters, including the Mohmand and Shinwari tribes, both located in southeastern Nangarhar. Sherzai's Kandahar-based militia did not follow him to Nangarhar.

The local population largely respected Governor Sherzai because of his efforts to promote development and reconstruction, especially in the capital city of Jalalabad.[4] He was dubbed "the Bulldozer" because of the many reconstruction projects he implemented. The local population widely acknowledged that most of the governor's reconstruction funds came from illegal tolls. They did not seem to mind the corruption,

Figure 1: Opium Cultivation in Nangarhar, 1994–2009 (in hectares)[8]

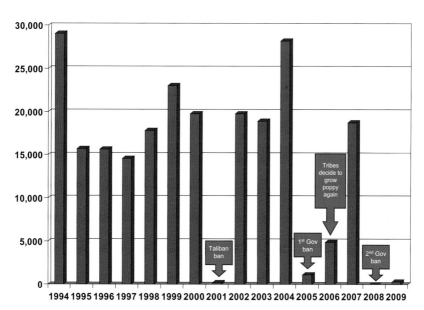

Poppy Cultivation in Nangarhar, 2004

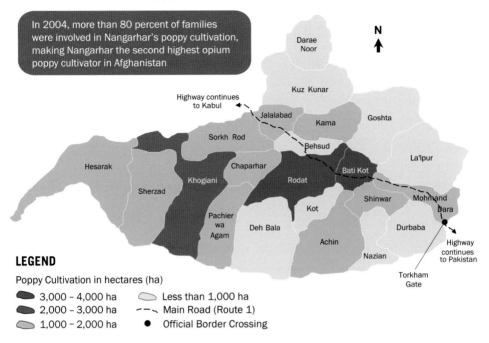

In 2004, more than 80 percent of families were involved in Nangarhar's poppy cultivation, making Nangarhar the second highest opium poppy cultivator in Afghanistan

LEGEND

Poppy Cultivation in hectares (ha)

- 3,000 – 4,000 ha
- 2,000 – 3,000 ha
- 1,000 – 2,000 ha
- Less than 1,000 ha
- – – Main Road (Route 1)
- ● Official Border Crossing

however, because many of them benefited from it. Governor Sherzai was voted "person of the year" in 2008 in a call-in radio poll and was briefly in the running for president before pulling out of the race in 2009.[5]

Governor Sherzai maintained close relationships with the PRT, Coalition forces, and nongovernmental organizations (NGOs), meeting with them at least several times a week. He also attended groundbreaking and grand opening ceremonies of development and reconstruction projects carried out by the PRT.

Bans on Opium Production

Nangarhar had a long history of opium poppy cultivation, typically ranking among the top three provinces in Afghanistan. Poppy cultivation fell in 2001 after a ban was imposed by the Taliban (see Figure 1). However, the Taliban's ban on opium poppy cultivation proved unsustainable and planting resumed even before the Taliban fell from power.[6] The opium trade later became one of largest sources of funding for the Taliban.[7]

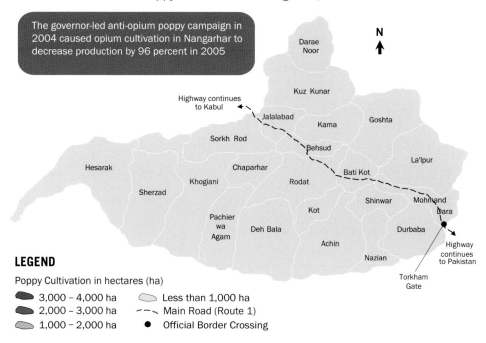

Poppy Cultivation in Nangarhar, 2005

The governor-led anti-opium poppy campaign in 2004 caused opium cultivation in Nangarhar to decrease production by 96 percent in 2005

LEGEND

Poppy Cultivation in hectares (ha)

- 3,000 – 4,000 ha
- 2,000 – 3,000 ha
- 1,000 – 2,000 ha
- Less than 1,000 ha
- - - - Main Road (Route 1)
- ● Official Border Crossing

While Nangarhar was once considered one of Afghanistan's "breadbaskets," problems with irrigation became a major hindrance to the productivity of local farmers. Decades of war in Afghanistan had destroyed most of the province's irrigation systems, making it difficult for rural farmers to access sufficient and reliable water supplies. Years of drought contributed to the shortages in the water supply, which affected what crops farmers were able to grow (e.g., wheat required more water and fertilizer than opium poppy).

In an effort to deter local farmers from continuing to grow opium poppy, the provincial government made two major attempts to eradicate poppy growth in Nangarhar.

First Attempt: 2004–2005 Ban

After a near-record cultivation for the province in 2004, when more than 80 percent of Nangarhari families were involved in opium poppy cultivation (see Map: Poppy Cultivation in Nangarhar, 2004), then-governor Haji Din Mohammed implemented a ban on opium poppy for the 2004–2005 growing season in accordance with President Karzai's anti-opium campaign.[8] The provincial government largely based its implementation on

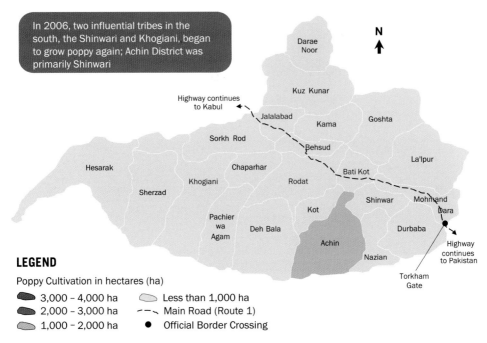

In 2006, two influential tribes in the south, the Shinwari and Khogiani, began to grow poppy again; Achin District was primarily Shinwari

LEGEND

Poppy Cultivation in hectares (ha)

- 3,000 – 4,000 ha
- 2,000 – 3,000 ha
- 1,000 – 2,000 ha
- Less than 1,000 ha
- – – ⌐ Main Road (Route 1)
- ● Official Border Crossing

what the Taliban had done during the 2000–2001 ban and placed emphasis on preventing farmers from planting the crop.[9] The governor threatened district-level government leaders by indicating that their jobs depended on the reduction of opium cultivation. At the start of the planting season in November, district administrators informed tribal leaders (who were responsible for poppy cultivation decisions in Nangarhar) of the poppy ban and paid them for their compliance. Tribal leaders were also promised development assistance in return for compliance with the ban.

After the information campaign during the planting season, the government proceeded with an eradication campaign during the harvest, destroying 1,860 hectares of opium poppy and arresting farmers.[10] Licit crops were occasionally destroyed in the process. Corruption was also a big problem. Many wealthier farmers were able to pay off eradicators to spare their crops.

Because of the ban, opium poppy cultivation in Nangarhar decreased by 96 percent in 2005 (see Figure 1 and Map: Poppy Cultivation in Nangarhar, 2005). U.S. officials claimed it was "the most significant victory in the battle against narcotics in Afghanistan."[11]

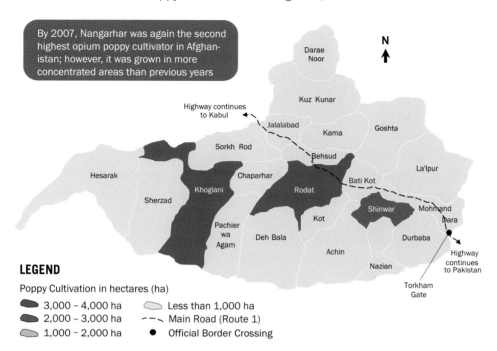

By 2007, Nangarhar was again the second highest opium poppy cultivator in Afghanistan; however, it was grown in more concentrated areas than previous years

LEGEND

Poppy Cultivation in hectares (ha)

3,000 – 4,000 ha   Less than 1,000 ha
2,000 – 3,000 ha   Main Road (Route 1)
1,000 – 2,000 ha   Official Border Crossing

However, while Nangarhar was considered an opium eradication success, the ban caused economic hardship and discontent among the population. As in other provinces, farmers in Nangarhar took loans from drug traffickers in the fall to plant their poppy crops. The traffickers then returned after the harvest to be repaid in poppy. Traffickers multiplied the debt if they were not repaid within a year. In 2005, the vast majority of farmers were not able to compensate for their income loss through other crops.[12] As a result, many farmers could not pay off their debts. Some reportedly repaid traffickers by selling their daughters into marriage, which also occurred during the Taliban opium ban.[13] The ban also had a deeper impact on the overall economy, as people had less disposable income to spend in markets and other industries.

In addition, the majority of farmers saw few rewards after complying with the poppy ban. Promises of alternative livelihoods and development projects for farmers were not fulfilled at expected levels. Only a small number of development projects found their way to the average farmer.

Development projects created some employment opportunities, but they did not compare to opportunities previously available through the opium crop. Cash-for-work programs—typically short-term manual labor—were thus perceived as insufficient since they did not pay farmers enough to make up their income losses.

Labor rates also affected income. Most of the opium was replaced by wheat, however, wheat requires less labor than opium—on average, 350 working days per hectare for opium versus 51 days per hectare for wheat.[14] Many workers who typically traveled to cultivating areas of Nangarhar suddenly found themselves out of work. Wage rates thus declined because of the surplus of available workers. As a result, many workers went into Pakistan to find employment.

The cultivation ban caused resentment toward the Coalition, which was seen as spearheading the eradication. People even threatened to provide support to the Taliban who passed through the area.[15]

Ultimately, the ban was unsustainable because farmers could not afford to uphold it for another year. They also claimed that the government had not kept its development promises. Two important tribes in the south, the Shinwari and Khogiani, collaborated and chose not to follow the government's opium ban for another year.[16] By 2006, opium poppy cultivation began to increase in remote parts of the province dominated by those two tribes (see Map: Poppy Cultivation in Nangarhar, 2006).

Achieving Poppy-Free Status: 2007–2008 Ban

In 2007, Nangarhar opium poppy cultivation increased by 285 percent (see Figure 1), making the province, once again, the second-highest cultivator in the country. Poppy cultivation, however, was concentrated in remote areas, which differed from the pattern in previous years (see Map: Poppy Cultivation in Nangarhar, 2007). More eradication was conducted in 2007 than any year before, inciting the highest number of eradication-related security incidents in the country.[17] U.S. military forces noticed a shift from attacks on Coalition forces to attacks on the ANSF, which were responsible for governor-led eradication in the province.

Despite his involvement with the drug trade in Kandahar, Governor Sherzai reportedly opposed poppy production in Nangarhar. During the fall of 2007, he launched a proactive anti-poppy campaign with the help of the Coalition using a three-pronged approach. First, the governor worked with local officials and the provincial council to help eliminate

Poppy Cultivation in Nangarhar, 2008

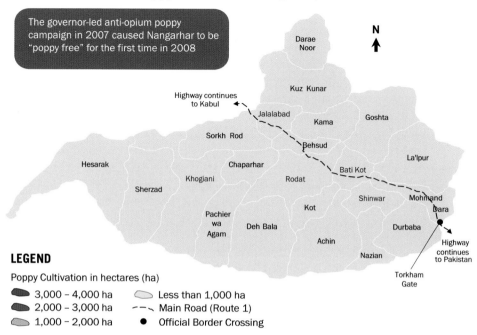

The governor-led anti-opium poppy campaign in 2007 caused Nangarhar to be "poppy free" for the first time in 2008

LEGEND

Poppy Cultivation in hectares (ha)

- 3,000 – 4,000 ha
- 2,000 – 3,000 ha
- 1,000 – 2,000 ha
- Less than 1,000 ha
- – – ˎ Main Road (Route 1)
- ● Official Border Crossing

poppy cultivation. Governor Sherzai threatened to remove local administrators from their positions if poppy grew in their districts and gained credibility when he removed three district governors. In turn, local officials engaged community leaders to emphasize the benefits of not growing the crop. As in previous campaigns, local leaders were paid for their compliance with the ban. With the help of the PRT, provincial officials and district committees then led a public information campaign to spread the anti-poppy message with the Coalition's help. Governor Sherzai promised to reward areas that reduced poppy cultivation with increased development assistance. As a result, tribal leaders all agreed not to grow poppy and not to provide anti-government fighters safe haven in their areas.[18]

Second, the new policy was strictly enforced. Unlike in previous eradication campaigns, if poppy fields were discovered, local leaders gave farmers the opportunity to eradicate the crop themselves. Governor Sherzai issued an ultimatum: "Plow up the poppy fields or go to jail."[19] If farmers refused, they were arrested. Those involved at the lower levels, such as farmers and low-level traffickers, received the most punishment. ANSF conducted the least amount of eradication in 2008 than in any other year.[20]

The Coalition chose to ignore some of the governor's more forceful persuasion methods. For example, he reportedly spread rumors that farmers' noncompliance would result in U.S. raids. Coalition forces had established a larger presence throughout the province in May 2007, and Governor Sherzai implied that their mandate was to enforce the anti-poppy campaign, even though that was not the case.[21]

Finally, by engaging with the local population, the provincial and district-level government learned more about what local communities needed. Governor Sherzai reportedly visited many districts himself. As a result, more people, particularly those from remote areas who had never interacted with government officials, became acquainted with the government.

Due to the governor's strong anti-poppy campaign, Nangarhar Province became designated "poppy free" for the first time in 2008 (see Figure 1 and Map: Poppy Cultivation in Nangarhar, 2008).[22] As many as 40,000 farming families received some kind of compensation for the loss of opium revenues.[23] Wheat prices also increased at the same time, giving farmers a viable crop alternative.

Under the Good Performers Initiative, provinces determined by the United Nations Office on Drugs and Crime (UNODC) to be "poppy free" received funds for development assistance. In 2008, Nangarhar received the maximum $10 million reward,[24] but the governor was not given direct access to these funds to ensure that the entire amount went toward reconstruction projects. Districts planned to use the money to improve the irrigation infrastructure.[25]

The Supporting Role of U.S. Forces

While the Coalition did not actively participate in the governor's eradication campaign (per command guidance), it did support the governor's efforts through public information campaigns and reconstruction projects. A second PRT, known as an agribusiness development team (ADT)—the first of its kind in Afghanistan—deployed to the province in February 2008 to augment the PRT and focus specifically on agriculture, because farming was the primary profession in the province. Projects included building grain mills and cool storage facilities, distributing seeds, advising farmers on farming techniques, and assessing and fixing water and power problems. The PRT and ADT were careful to deliver on their promises.

The Coalition also worked with the provincial government and the provincial community council to create the "Nangarhar, Inc." economic business plan. The interagency plan consisted of quick-impact projects aimed at leveraging the governor's poppy eradication success during the growing season.[26] For example, in the district of Rodat, the PRT and counternarcotics advisory team (CNAT) dug canals, known as *karezes*, to increase local irrigation capabilities and paved roads to help farmers get their crops to market, while the ADT encouraged and taught farmers marketing techniques and ways to grow new onion varieties. Due to these coordinated efforts, some districts, such as Rodat, experienced record onion sales. Farmers were even able to make more money on onions than they had on poppy.[27]

While the PRT and ADT focused on reconstruction and development, military forces kept a relatively low profile in the province as they helped build local Afghan capacity to provide security. U.S. military forces gained a larger presence in May 2007, and, as more forces arrived in the area, the number of clashes with insurgents increased.

The new soldiers worked closely with the Afghan National Police (ANP)—conducting daily joint patrols at all hours—and with a police chief who was largely respected by the population and Governor Sherzai (unlike the governor's predecessor, Haji Din Mohammed). The ANSF took the lead in every search and arrest, and patrolled the capital city without the help of U.S. soldiers. Yet while the ANP controlled the situation in Jalalabad, they lacked manpower and resources in many districts—especially in remote areas— and rarely left their posts or district centers. The Coalition set up two major law enforcement training programs—district-level immersion and focused district development—in the province. While police were in training, the governor pressured tribal leaders to be responsible for security in their own areas.

In 2008, the Nangarhar Joint Provincial Coordination Center (JPCC) was established to coordinate actions between the Coalition and local Afghan security forces.[28] Locals were able to dial an emergency phone number to contact the center for help in situations ranging from natural disaster emergencies to insurgent activity. The JPCC was co-located with the ANP Headquarters and had representatives from the military forces, Afghan National Army (ANA), and Afghan Border Police (ABP) on site to help respond to emergencies effectively. At least once a week, U.S. soldiers met with the ANSF at the center to coordinate actions and exchange information. In effect, this helped put the ANA and ANP in control of providing security for the province, especially in Jalalabad. U.S. and Afghan military forces also met with Pakistani border police to discuss border activity.

The PRT, ADT, and military forces—collectively dubbed Team Nangarhar— were all head-quartered on the same base. Living on the same base eased coordination among the different teams.

Conclusion

Nangarhar is different from other provinces in Afghanistan's south and east due to its relatively benign security situation and functioning government, which allowed U.S. forces to enable the Afghans to take the lead in providing security. Because the Taliban did not have a stronghold in the province, an influential governor and a strong police chief were able to work together to secure areas. The U.S. Army battalion in Nangarhar took a supporting role in training the ANP and creating the JPCC to improve coordina-tion. In addition, the battalion worked with the province's PRT and ADT to distribute aid and complete reconstruction projects in line with the provincial government's develop-ment plan. Unity of effort was key to their success.

The success of the anti-poppy campaign in Nangarhar resulted largely from strong po-litical will. In 2007, Governor Sherzai, who had once been a notorious warlord in Kan-dahar, became responsible for a successful campaign to eliminate opium poppy in Nangarhar. His pressure and commitment were crucial to the success of the overall campaign. Even though the Coalition chose to ignore some of his more firm-handed tactics, he was ultimately successful in working with local leaders to reduce poppy cul-tivation in the province and in increasing development as a reward.

The 2007 campaign incorporated lessons from prior bans, including the importance of economic sustainability. As he did with the ban in 2004, Governor Sherzai emphasized the positive benefits to the public of growing alternative crops, paid off tribal leaders for their compliance during cultivation, and threatened leaders who did not comply. How-ever, this time, he enforced his threats by firing district governors when poppy was dis-covered in their areas and by making widespread arrests. He also allowed farmers to eradicate their own poppies, compensated families for the loss of their opium revenues, and provided them with viable crop alternatives. The price of wheat increased that year, providing families with an equivalent income. Through supporting PRT and ADT development projects, the local populace saw an effect in their daily lives. Some of the smallest projects had the biggest impact.

Governor Sherzai's successful anti-poppy campaign would not have worked without security. Nangarhar's relatively benign security situation allowed farmers to travel to market their goods more easily than farmers in more dangerous provinces, such as Helmand, could.

Unlike the many sharecroppers in the south, tribes in eastern Afghanistan have an important decision-making role in determining what crops to grow. By paying off and securing the compliance of the tribes, Governor Sherzai was able to guarantee low poppy cultivation levels.

Finally, farmers in Nangarhar were provided with viable crop alternatives, such as onions and wheat, allowing families to earn an equal or greater income. In 2008, the price of wheat surpassed that of opium poppy. However, wheat prices decreased the following year, so its long-term sustainability remains in question.

U.S. Army Special Forces Team
Kandahar and Zabul, 2003–2005

This vignette describes the efforts of a small U.S. Army Special Forces (SF) team over the course of two very different deployments.

During its first tour, from September 2003 to March 2004, the team was part of a large, centrally directed assault force based at Kandahar Airfield that focused entirely on kill-capture missions and large-scale sweeps. These operations yielded few results, in part because most Taliban had either fled or been killed in 2003.

During its second deployment, from June 2004 to January 2005, the team focused on small-scale counterinsurgency with little central direction in a remote area of Zabul Province. Through careful local engagement and economic investment, the SF team built a base of support in an adamantly pro-Taliban area.

September 2003 to March 2004: Direct Action

During its first deployment to Afghanistan, Operational Detachment Alpha (ODA) focused on high-value targeting. It was based at Kandahar Airfield, a sprawling Soviet-built base outside of Kandahar City that was the headquarters of numerous military units.

The team was part of a larger force that concentrated entirely on counterterrorism and direct action—mainly airborne raids. It conducted no governance or development activities, engagement with the population, or anything else long term. Nor did the team conduct any training, equipping, or advise-and-assist operations.

Nearly all of the team's missions turned out to be "dry holes"—that is, operations that saw no enemy contact. Many were airborne raids that targeted Taliban leaders and

---

Unless otherwise noted, this vignette is based on extensive interviews with the team's commanding officer, in Monterey, California, on 12 October 2009. All information—as well as perspectives on operations and the areas mentioned—comes from these interviews.

arms caches. Some of these raids mistakenly targeted Afghan civilians. The team did not find a single insurgent leader during its first tour and saw almost no fighting.

These operations were largely ineffective in part because there were few insurgents to be found in 2003 and 2004 and also because information was frequently old or faulty. Afghans often fed SF units false information to manipulate them. The distances were so great and the terrain so difficult that it was usually impossible for SF units to go into remote areas undetected; by the time they arrived, insurgent leaders (if there were any) had fled.

The team's battalion was relatively centralized, with little in the way of distributed operations (i.e., decentralized execution, latitude to subordinate units). Many missions were battalion-level sweep operations, some of them involving hundreds of Afghan Militia Forces (AMF) loyal to the governor of Kandahar.

One of these large-scale sweep operations was in the Deh Chopan Valley, a remote area in Zabul Province, during October 2003. The assault demonstrates many of the problems with direct action and battalion-level operations in remote areas of Afghanistan.

The SF battalion knew almost nothing about Deh Chopan prior to the operation, except what it had been told by militia fighters who themselves knew little about the area. The battalion had no up-to-date maps and relied entirely on the AMF to lead the way. Their information on the supposed existence of a large enemy force was more than two months old by the time the operation began.

The plan was to advance on the area from four directions using a combination of U.S. forces and Afghan militiamen. It was a movement-to-contact operation; the idea was to push in by land and air from multiple directions and seek immediate engagement with the enemy. The battalion did not intend to do cordon-and-knock operations (i.e., establish an outer perimeter and search compounds), much less establish a permanent presence, hold the area, and build institutions.

It was to be a massive sweep operation carried out mostly by indigenous militias. These militiamen were primarily loyal to Gul Agha Sherzai, the warlord governor of Kandahar Province and a member of the Barakzai tribe [for more on Sherzai, see Vignette 6]. The people from Deh Chopan came from a different tribe.

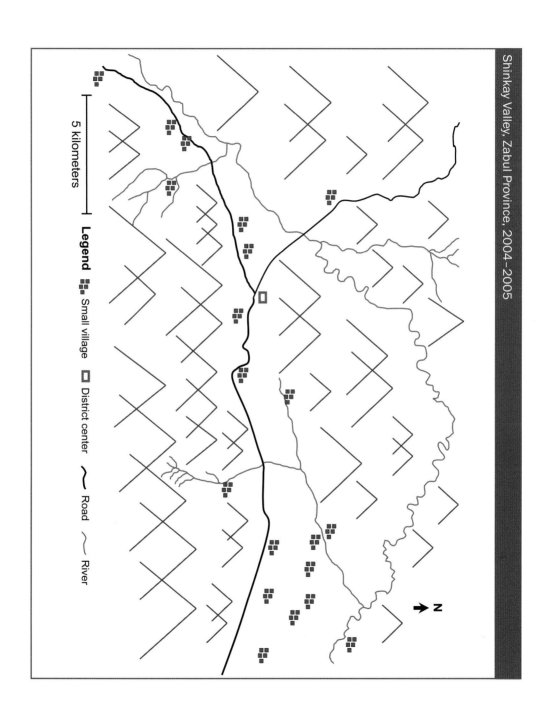

Shinkay Valley, Zabul Province, 2004–2005

5 kilometers

Legend

- Small village
- □ District center
- ⌇ Road
- ⌇ River

N

The AMF engaged in widespread looting during the operation. They were poorly organized and undisciplined. SF units following after handed out money to many of those looted by the militiamen.

As the SF and AMF moved into the valley, they saw busloads of Afghan men of fighting age driving in the opposite direction. SF units stopped some of these vehicles, but the men inside were unarmed and all had a story; there was no clear indication that they were Taliban. Many were insurgents, but many were also local people keen to avoid the fighting.

The operation resulted in very little contact with the Taliban. The insurgents had hidden their weapons and either fled or gone underground by the time the SF and AMF arrived in Deh Chopan. One of the SF teams and some AMF set up a firebase in the valley. After about a month of quiet, they left. Many of the insurgents then returned to Deh Chopan. Using typical guerrilla methods, they withdrew, waited for the occupying force to leave, and then returned.

The operation in Deh Chopan was the largest of numerous direct action missions carried out by the SF team highlighted in this vignette from September 2003 to March 2004. It is unclear what, if any, effect these large-scale combat operations had on the insurgency, much less on the capacity of the Afghan government to stand on its own.

June 2004 to January 2005: Counterinsurgency

The team spent its second deployment to Afghanistan from June 2004 to January 2005 in a counterinsurgency role while based out of a small outpost in Shinkay District, an extremely remote and mountainous area in Zabul Province. The team was responsible for the eastern half of Zabul, from the Ring Road south and east all the way to the border with Pakistan—an enormous, sparsely populated area with mountainous terrain.

The team's battalion headquarters adopted a highly decentralized, indirect approach, with considerable autonomy given to each SF team to engage with the local population, train indigenous forces, collect intelligence, and conduct raids as need be. The battalion's many teams were dispersed into small firebases across southern Afghanistan, many of them in extremely remote areas. The battalion focused almost entirely on counterinsurgency and conducted relatively little counterterrorism or direct action.

Shinkay Firebase was an exposed mud compound with minimal fortifications, guarded mainly by Afghan soldiers and militiamen. The Shinkay district government consisted of only a few local police and a district governor housed in a small building near the firebase. The district governor apparently cooperated with the Taliban, and the insurgents mostly left him alone.

The team inherited two companies of Afghan soldiers trained by a previous SF team. Most were ethnic Hazaras and Tajiks, and their officers were mainly northern Pashtuns. There were also about 150 to 200 Afghan mercenaries, most of them from Kandahar. These militiamen guarded the base; they were not allowed to go on offensive operations.

The team's influence did not extend more than 12 to 15 kilometers beyond its firebase. The farther a village was from the base, the less influence the team had, and the more the Taliban were in control. These were small villages, most of them less than ten mud-walled compounds, and very spread out. Beyond 15 kilometers in every direction was a vast area where the team almost never went. U.S. forces had no presence on the other side of the mountain range toward the border with Pakistan where insurgents moved freely and controlled many populated areas.

The Taliban wielded considerable influence across this vast area, including the areas immediately around the firebase, which was dominated by Pashtuns from the Hotak tribe, part of the Ghilzai confederation—the same tribe as the Taliban's supreme leader, Mullah Omar. Many hardcore Taliban fighters and senior leaders came from this area and continued to operate there after the U.S. invasion.

Most of the Hotak villages were adamantly pro-Taliban and resistant to any government presence. For them, the Taliban presence was a way of life. Even under Taliban rule, they mainly governed themselves. The U.S. invasion had little effect on their situation. Small numbers of Taliban operatives continued to provide useful services with minimal corruption or repression. They provided security, prevented extortion, punished criminals, and adjudicated disputes between families and clans. There was little evidence that insurgents were intimidating Hotak villages.

The Taliban had anywhere from five to 15 operatives in most major villages or clusters of villages. They moved around on motorcycles, usually unarmed, and operated an effective intelligence network. They dispersed and fled in advance of most raids and cordon-and-knock operations. Yet they also consolidated forces to attack government installations and ambush U.S. patrols. Insurgents based in different villages would gather in one location, carry out their attack, and then disperse again.

The local people did not seek protection from American or Afghan forces. They were openly hostile to the idea of Afghan police or army garrisons within the confines of their villages. When asked, village leaders said they did not want to be responsible for the security of Afghan army or police checkpoints, which would attract insurgent attacks and cause divisions within their communities. Despite the presence of Taliban operatives near the firebase, the team carried out few raids within its sphere of influence for fear of alienating the population.

The only exceptions were a few openly pro-government villages, all of them inhabited by non-Hotak tribes with connections to the Karzai government. These villages contained large police garrisons, which often came under attack.

The SF team participated in a nearby shura every Tuesday morning, which included elders from surrounding villages. Local elders asked for money and projects from the team and complained about the heavy-handed tactics of previous units. The area's leaders carried out most of their business outside the shura in one-on-one meetings. The team allowed local people to come and go freely on the base. About 120 locals were employed on the base. Many also came to receive free medical care from the team's doctor, who was trained in surgery, general medicine, dentistry, and veterinary medicine. The team also traveled to distant villages to treat the sick. Known as medical civic assistance programs, or MEDCAPs, these missions often yielded valuable information and goodwill.

The team (and the Afghan soldiers under its command) was tied in closely to the local economy. It became an important source of revenue for the surrounding population. The SF team bought nearly all its food in nearby markets and used only local labor, all purchased at local rates. The soldiers also employed a local cook to prepare their meals. The one item contracted from outside was heavy equipment, which was not available locally.

The team avoided working through local contractors, especially those who spoke English (indicating that they were experienced at manipulating U.S. forces) or were from outside the area. The team learned early on that dispensing money through a single individual made this person unduly powerful and encouraged corruption. Local contractors tended to hire only from their clan, creating resentment among others. U.S. soldiers paid wages directly to workers and purchased goods themselves from the local market. When hiring laborers, the team went to the weekly shura and asked for workers from each village leader.

Insurgents operating in these villages reportedly carried out few or no attacks on the SF team, for fear of alienating the locals. The one major exception was a roadside bomb attack later traced to a rival clan that had reaped no benefits from the presence of U.S. forces. This clan apparently felt threatened by the growing prosperity of those villages closer to the firebase.

Over time, the local population came to value the economic benefits that the presence of U.S. forces brought and worked to ensure the security of the base and its surroundings. The people did this despite their tribal connections to the Taliban and their tendency to support its political program and give refuge to its fighters.

Conclusion

During its first tour in Afghanistan, from September 2003 to March 2004, the SF team learned that direct action did not always work, especially against insurgents in remote mountain areas where there were no Coalition forces and very little accurate information.

Battalion-level sweep operations proved ineffective, both at capturing or killing insurgents and at projecting influence. The operation in Deh Chopan achieved little, except to alienate the people there. The operation met with few insurgents and caused considerable harm to the local population. The operation was slow, clumsy, and ill-informed. Insurgents had plenty of time to flee, leaving innocent people to bear the brunt of the attack.

The team learned some sobering lessons about indigenous militias. Afghan mercenaries engaged in widespread looting as they moved through Deh Chopan. These forces may have put an "Afghan face" on the operation, but they were not native to Deh Chopan. They abused the population as if Deh Chopan was an enemy nation. By allying with these militias and facilitating their predatory behavior, the SF battalion helped sow enduring enmity against U.S. forces.

The SF team also learned not to trust information unless it had been carefully vetted. The Afghan militia commanders and other individuals repeatedly fed false information to the SF battalion, leading it on fruitless missions, some of which led to civilian deaths.

The team's second deployment could not have been more different. The team's experiences from June 2004 to January 2005 demonstrated that counterinsurgency could work, even when the population was inclined to support the enemy; the solution was to bring money into the community while doing no harm.

The SF team used its funds strategically to tie the health of the local economy to the continued presence of Coalition forces. Economic interest trumped ideology and tribal connections. It is unclear whether the SF team won hearts or minds or whether doing so was even possible. What the team did do was link the interests of the community to the interests of the SF team and the Afghan soldiers under its command.

The soldiers learned early on that money was power, especially in a place as poor and rural as Afghanistan. The team dispensed funds as patronage, much like a patronage-based political machine. It gave money directly to laborers to provide jobs and spread these funds evenly among the area's 20 or so villages.

The team learned that giving small amounts of money was better than giving large sums; it did not take much to achieve desired effects. The soldiers were careful to pay local market rates for labor and goods. The team ended up spending only a fraction of its allotted funds.

The team avoided funneling money through contractors or a single local leader. It learned early on that doing so created power brokers who used their influence to benefit their constituents at the expense of others, causing other communities to resent the presence of Coalition forces. Cutting out middlemen increased the amount of influence the SF team was able to glean from the money it spent, while minimizing corruption.

The local population protected the SF team, not the other way around. The soldiers were able to build such a strong and reliable network of support around their firebase that they did not require fortifications and could move around easily with little risk of attack—even though Shinkay was a notoriously pro-Taliban area.

During its second deployment, the team focused its activity on a relatively small area around its firebase. The team recognized that its ability to influence the population diminished the farther out it went. Rather than spread its efforts across a wider area, the team focused its energies on 20 or so nearby villages. The team avoided patrols except where its presence was welcomed and did not establish Afghan army checkpoints except in the few villages that clearly supported such a presence.

The team learned that local people did not necessarily want to be protected by Coalition forces, whether American or Afghan. Permanent garrisons and checkpoints attracted insurgent attacks and threatened the autonomy of fiercely independent, self-governing villages. This was particularly true in remote areas such as Shinkay, where the Taliban's presence was never particularly intrusive. Where locals opposed the presence of soldiers and police, bases and patrols tended to strengthen the Taliban by providing it with opportunities to win popular support.

The human and physical terrain in Afghanistan vary widely from one area to the next, especially in remote mountain valleys. During the team's second tour, the SF battalion headquarters gave its teams considerable autonomy, allowing them to adapt to different local conditions.

Finally, in Shinkay, the people protected U.S. forces. The soldiers depended on local support for their security. Once the neighboring villages came to see the value of the SF presence, the team faced little risk of attack in the surrounding area.

Three U.S. Army Special Forces Teams
Kunar and Nuristan, 2004–2005

From June 2004 to October 2005, three U.S. Army Special Forces (SF) teams rotated through northern Kunar and Nuristan in remote northeastern Afghanistan on six- to seven-month tours. Their operations set the groundwork for the conventional units that followed.

The region's people live in isolated mountain valleys and have been fiercely protective of their autonomy. It was one of the few areas of Afghanistan that the Soviet army failed to penetrate in the 1980s. The Taliban had little influence there, even at the height of their power.

The area is close to the border with Pakistan. Beyond that are the inaccessible areas of Dir and Bajaur in northwestern Pakistan, where the al-Qaeda leadership was reportedly hiding at the time.

A major part of the mission for these small teams was to collect intelligence on al-Qaeda and associated groups and target their leaders. Yet for these teams operating in the distant reaches of northeast Afghanistan, developing relationships with local people and building indigenous forces was an essential task in order to collect the information needed to target terrorist leaders as well as simply to stay alive.

This vignette focuses on three consecutive SF teams. The first was in Kunar and Nuristan from June to December 2004. The second was there from December 2004 to June 2005, and the third, from June to October 2005.

June to December 2004

In the summer of 2004, an SF team was sent to northern Kunar and Nuristan to target leaders of al-Qaeda and the Hizbul-e-Islami Gulbuddin (HiG). At that time, much of the

This vignette is based entirely on interviews with the leaders of these three teams.

al-Qaeda leadership was believed to be hiding just across the border in the far north-western reaches of Pakistan.

The SF team established its firebase at Naray, a small village along the Kunar River in the far northern corner of the province. The village consisted of just a handful of forti-fied compounds and a few poppy fields along a ridge overlooking the river. During the first few weeks, the team patrolled into nearby villages to gather information and ac-quaint themselves with the villagers. Before long, the team began pushing north on multiday missions into Nuristan where the HiG's influence was strong.

It took days for the team to get to Nuristan's remote and isolated mountain valleys. The roads were poor, and many villages were accessible only by foot. Most people lived in tributary valleys branching off the area's only drivable road. If the team used its vehicles at all, it was to drive to the mouth of a mountain valley and then hike the rest of the way.

The team's influence, in terms of its ability to effectively protect the population and se-cure its cooperation, did not extend more than 1 or 2 kilometers north and south of the firebase. It took as long as seven hours just to hike to the observation posts overlook-ing the firebase and visit the villages nearby. The team set up a small base to the north, but insurgents attacked the position relentlessly, forcing the team to close it down.

The team soon learned that the best and perhaps only way to gather useful information was to go on three- to seven-day foot patrols into the mountains. SF and the Afghan sol-diers patrolling with them ate, drank, and slept in villages along the way. They had to pack lightly if they hoped to cross ridgelines as high as 12,000 feet.

Before moving into a village, the team would set up a cordon outside the town. Once in-side, it was a matter of honor for the elders to ensure the soldiers' security. The team was attacked only once while inside a populated area, and nearly all attacks on the sol-diers occurred away from populated areas. Some of these were sophisticated attacks from multiple directions.

The team was able to collect information on the enemy, but effectively targeting insur-gent or terrorist leaders proved exceedingly difficult. It was nearly impossible for U.S. forces to move around the region's remote mountain valleys without word spreading ahead of their arrival. Most insurgents managed to flee or hide long before the soldiers arrived. The insurgents had networks of informers throughout the region that provided early warning. Each village also had lookouts who watched for outsiders passing through their territory. The same was true of valleys such as the Korangal to the south, where heavy-handed sweep operations netted few insurgents and made many enemies.

The team learned a great deal about local tribal conflicts and historical rivalries. These conflicts were complex; many revolved around water. Feuding clans mined paths to the river and lobbed mortars at one another. Heavily armed men with field rations hiked days to raid villages in neighboring valleys. The team occasionally came across these raiding parties, but left them alone for fear of getting involved in local feuds. The team held shuras with elders from Kamdesh and Gowardesh and tried to broker agreements between rival clans. The team avoided taking sides or using force to restrain one side or the other. Insurgent leaders exploited these divisions, arming rival groups and using local grudges to make inroads into remote communities.

National identity or loyalty to anyone outside one's clan or village was almost unknown. Each valley was like its own country, dotted with isolated and self-contained villages. Many people in these towns had never left their village; anyone from outside was a foreigner to be treated with mistrust. Past governments had done little or nothing for these villages, and they were accustomed to living without outside support or interference. The idea of direct rule by provincial or district officials was a foreign concept.

Many villages were reluctant to cooperate with the team because of strong insurgent influence, the belief that U.S. forces would not remain long, and an inherent distrust of any outside force. The villagers mostly hedged their bets and played both sides. Many villages were openly hostile and organized attacks on the team as it passed through their territory, not because they necessarily had anything against the United States, but because they viewed the presence of any outside armed group as a threat to their security and autonomy. The first time the team went to Kamdesh, people fled, thinking that the Americans were Russians coming to destroy their villages.

The team was not tasked or resourced to bolster the government, build local forces, engage with the population, or carry out reconstruction efforts. Locals often came to the firebase to ask for help, but addressing local problems was not a priority mission.

Nonetheless, the team devoted much of its effort to engaging the population and training and mentoring indigenous forces. Regular patrols, reconstruction projects, shuras, and other efforts to engage local people were key to gathering intelligence, not just against al-Qaeda but also against other insurgents keen to attack the firebase and soldiers on patrol. The only way to develop reliable sources was to build local support.

The SF team was too small and isolated to protect its firebase without reliable and well-trained Afghan soldiers and militiamen to serve as force multipliers. Afghan troops went on missions, helping to protect the team as it moved on foot through remote and dangerous areas. A force of about 100 Afghan militiamen recruited from nearby villages guarded the base and patrolled nearby. The team learned that the insurgents, many of whom were local youths keen to target foreign forces, were reluctant to fire at local guards.

December 2004 to June 2005

A second team took over in December 2004 and continued the efforts of the previous team, with few apparent changes. This second team pushed out frequently on multiday foot patrols through the mountains, staying in local villages and trying to gather useful information to target and disrupt insurgents believed to be associated with al-Qaeda.

Like its predecessor, the team had little trouble finding people to talk to in the area's many remote villages. Yet its targeting efforts met with little success. It was nearly impossible for the team to take insurgent leaders by surprise, given their robust intelligence network and the difficulty of the terrain.

The team expanded its sphere of influence further around the firebase through local patrols and small reconstruction projects. The team started several road improvement projects near the base, repaired some small bridges, and finished a clinic begun during the previous team's tour.

The team developed a closer relationship with the local police chief at Bari Kowt and started a program to help train the small force of 10 to 15 policemen. Over time, the police began moving out of Bari Kowt and into far-flung villages. The relationship was sometimes strained, however, as the SF team suspected the police of maintaining links with the insurgents.

The soldiers forged an agreement with several large villages in Kamdesh that agreed to hand over some of their weapons. The agreement was difficult to enforce, however, because Kamdesh was more than seven hours from the firebase, five hours by road plus two hours hiking through the mountains. The team only went there three or four times; it was the farthest north the team ever ventured. Whether the Kamdeshis really meant to honor the agreement was never clear, as a small group of U.S. Marines and Afghan soldiers went to Kamdesh in late January 2005 to recover some of the promised weapons, and the convoy was ambushed from three sides while driving back through a narrow canyon. Three Afghan soldiers were killed.

June 2005 to October 2005

In June 2005, a third SF team was rotated in. By mid-2005, the SF command in Afghanistan was considering closing down Firebase Naray. The position was extremely isolated and increasingly difficult to secure. It was surrounded by mountains, and the road south was unsafe and often washed out because of floods. Roadside bomb incidents increased in 2005, forcing U.S. forces off the roads and restricting the extent of their influence.

The team tried to rectify this situation by working to secure the road between the provincial capital at Asadabad to the south and the firebase at Naray. It organized and funded local militias in villages along the route, with each militia responsible for a different section. The team also threatened to hold villages responsible for attacks along their stretch of the road. After four months, there were few ambushes or roadside bombs between Naray and the provincial capital at Asadabad, about 50 kilometers to the south.

By October 2005, the three consecutive SF teams had established a persistent presence around the firebase at Naray and projected sufficient influence beyond the firebase to make it possible for a larger conventional force to operate there in later years.

Yet U.S. forces remained largely unwelcome in the small tributary valleys of Nuristan to the north. The only area of Nuristan where U.S. forces had some reliable support was Bari Kowt, a border town that made a lot of money from commerce with Pakistan, and it, too, was unsafe. There was only so much that a small team of U.S. soldiers and a company or two of Afghans could do to clear and hold a vast area with such difficult human and physical terrain.

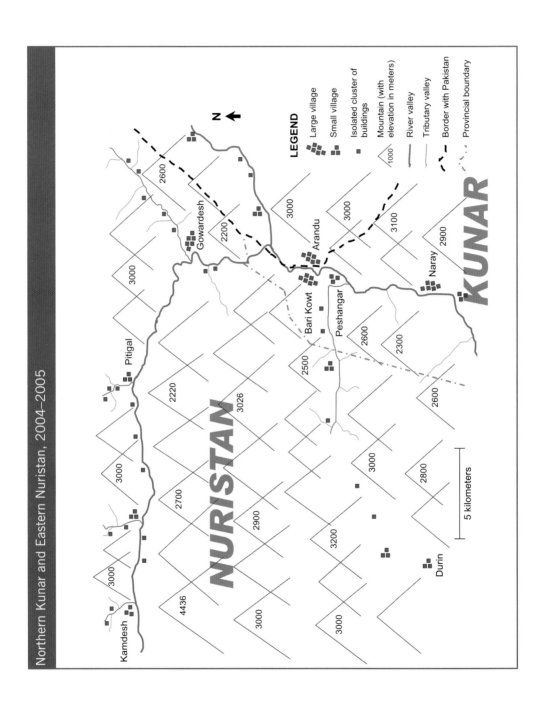

Northern Kunar and Eastern Nuristan, 2004–2005

NURISTAN

KUNAR

Kamdesh

Pitigal

Gowardesh

Bari Kowt

Peshangar

Arandu

Naray

Durin

4436

3000

3000

2700

2900

3000

3200

3000

2220

3026

2900

3000

3000

2500

2600

2300

2800

2600

2600

2200

2600

3000

3000

3100

2900

N

5 kilometers

LEGEND

Large village

Small village

Isolated cluster of buildings

1000 Mountain (with elevation in meters)

River valley

Tributary valley

Border with Pakistan

Provincial boundary

Conclusion

The terrain and distances in northern Kunar and eastern Nuristan imposed near-insurmountable obstacles to everything the SF teams attempted to do. Outside forces found it impossible to move through the region's mountain valleys undetected. As a result, kill-capture missions proved difficult and the risk of catastrophic ambushes remained high. The team's influence was limited to villages near the firebase, while insurgents roamed free in the areas beyond.

The region's population was isolated, self-governing, and mistrustful of outsiders. Government was nonexistent. Many attacks on U.S. and Afghan troops could be attributed to well-armed local youth keen to fire at any foreign force passing through their territory. Insurgent groups associated with al-Qaeda easily exploited this hostility to foreign influence. The three SF teams learned to maintain a light footprint and operate below the radar screen lest they inflame the population's xenophobic tendencies. Violence increased in later years with the arrival of large conventional army battalions with a more imposing and overt presence.

Frequent multiday foot patrols into the mountains proved essential to gathering useful information. SF and the Afghan soldiers under their command hiked through valleys and over ridgelines, eating, drinking, and sleeping in villages along the way and talking to local people. Though the population did not necessarily welcome the presence of U.S. forces, village leaders offered them sanctuary in accordance with local traditions. On the contrary, large-scale sweep operations like those in the Korangal Valley farther south (in which the SF teams at Naray sometimes participated) alienated local people, rarely netted insurgents, and were generally counterproductive.

The SF soldiers also raised and mentored indigenous forces in order to protect the firebase and provide additional security while on patrol beyond Naray. There was little that an SF team could do by itself, however well trained and adequately equipped. To operate effectively and stay alive in such remote and dangerous areas, SF had to work with Afghan forces and conduct traditional counterinsurgency operations, such as foot patrols, engagements with key leaders, and reconstruction projects, in addition to targeting terrorist leaders.

U.S. Army Special Forces Team
Kandahar, 2003–2004

This vignette describes the efforts of a U.S. Army Special Forces (SF) team over the course of two deployments—October 2003 to January 2004 and June to November 2004—in the city of Kandahar in southern Afghanistan.

The team operated from a compound in Kandahar City once used by Mullah Omar. The team's battalion headquarters was at Kandahar Airfield on the outskirts of the city. The overall focus of the battalion and its SF teams was on raids and large-scale kill-capture missions. Counterinsurgency was not a priority mission.

Nonetheless, the team focused much of its energy on engaging the city's population and conducting other counterinsurgency-related tasks. Kandahar City in 2003 was quite safe, its population openly supportive of U.S. forces. The soldiers moved around with little fear of attack, building relationships with local leaders.

When the team arrived for its second tour, however, it found that the environment and mood of Kandahar City had changed dramatically. Violence was on the rise. New units had adopted a more imposing and overtly military posture and had allowed relationships with local people to fray. Continuing raids and other combat operations contributed to growing tensions.

October 2003 to January 2004: Relationship Building

During its first deployment in Kandahar from October 2003 to January 2004, the team engaged constantly with the population. The soldiers met many of the city's leaders and focused on relationship building and development projects.

This vignette is based on extensive interviews with the team commander in Monterey, California, on 12 October 2009.

The team's mission was to conduct special operations. They received little or no strategic guidance or directives on counterinsurgency. The push from higher headquarters was for direct action and armed reconnaissance, that is, movement-to-contact. However, the team's activities also involved a notable amount of nonkinetic activity.

On its own initiative with little direction from higher headquarters, the team met frequently with President Hamid Karzai's brother, Ahmed Wali Karzai. The soldiers went to the Karzai family's house every few weeks for dinner. They met frequently with Governor Pashtuni, who had replaced Governor Sherzai as the head of the provincial government.

In 2003, Kandahar City was a safe and permissive environment for the SF team. The soldiers often walked the streets without helmets or weapons. They did so intentionally to maintain a low threat posture during their numerous interactions with local people. They shopped in the bazaar and ate at local restaurants and in the homes of prominent leaders. They met with the police chief and other city officials several times a week.

Some time into the team's deployment, units from the 10th Mountain Division arrived and conducted presence patrols in the city, which usually consisted of driving through the streets in armored vehicles, often pointing their guns at the population. For the SF team, the threatening posture of these patrols was counterproductive.

The team was not aware of any other U.S. officials working with Afghan government leaders in Kandahar and implementing reconstruction projects, even though the city welcomed development and political engagement. There was a large U.S. military presence at Kandahar Airfield, but only the SF team worked on development projects, such as restoring local schools. The team worked closely with several nongovernmental organizations in the city.

The team learned a great deal about the city's political dynamics. Each neighborhood was ruled by a group of elders from that neighborhood. There were three main power brokers in the city: the governor, the chief of police, and the Afghan Militia Forces (AMF) commander. The three fought constantly and rarely agreed on issues. The Afghan Militia Forces were controlled by warlords outside the provincial government. The SF team rented them out on occasion and trained them for use during specific operations.

The team conducted a few small raids, usually cordon-and-knocks, to detain Taliban leaders passing through. The team was also involved in some battalion-level sweep operations. These were large movement-to-contact operations that involved substantial numbers of forces pushing through an area and then leaving, the idea being to net large numbers of enemy fighters in a single operation. These sweeps met with little success—the insurgents easily fled and then returned when U.S. forces left.

June to November 2004: A Changing Environment

When the team returned for its second tour in June 2004, the situation in Kandahar City had changed dramatically. Violence, including ambushes on SF soldiers, was on the rise. U.S. forces had stepped up raids and other combat operations, which caused widespread resentment in and around Kandahar.

The team attempted to conduct the same activities it had during its first deployment, but found it more difficult now that violence was increasing. Bases were rocketed, bombs exploded inside the city, and grenades were thrown at U.S. patrols. The Taliban began moving back into the city, and public hostility toward the United States grew. There was also a steady increase in insurgent intimidation and night letters. The United Nations building and a school were hit by car bombs. The Taliban warned girls not to leave their homes.

Because the relationship between the city and the military had changed, casual dress with nonthreatening kit was no longer allowed for Coalition forces. U.S. soldiers wore body armor, helmets, combat equipment, and carried rifles at meetings and inside people's homes, putting barriers between themselves and the population. Many Afghan leaders, who believed it was a matter of honor to protect their guests, were offended by these practices.

The increase in violence coincided with a number of changes in the operating environment. Units from the 101st Airborne Division had replaced units from 10th Mountain Division. Special forces no longer controlled all U.S. forces in their areas of operation; this authority had passed to conventional units. The SF team was also no longer the main point of contact with the governor and other high-level officials.

In 2004, the Afghan Militia Forces were disbanded, and U.S. forces were no longer allowed to work with them. They remained as powerful as before, but lost their official status and became outsiders. There was little effort to disarm or reintegrate the militias. SF units were ordered to stop paying militiamen, who guarded SF bases and went along on operations. Many of these militiamen began attacking U.S. forces, including the SF team they had once worked for. The warlords remained powerful but were no longer working with SF or the government.

There were few official security forces to fill the vacuum left by the militias. Kandahar had police, but the SF team was not allowed to assist or train them. Police training was part of the mission of the UN and the State Department and was not to be undertaken by U.S. military forces. Several hundred police were deployed to Kandahar City but were not well trained or adequately supervised. Police corruption and extortion were rampant.

Conclusion

During its first tour in the city of Kandahar from October 2003 to January 2004, the SF team was the main U.S. presence in the city. The team focused on the population, building relationships and assisting with development projects. The team met with the city's official leaders often and worked through issues with them. Kandahar was a safe place with a largely positive outlook toward President Karzai, the United States, and the future. The team approached the people in a nonthreatening way, communicated with them frequently, and helped to maintain security in the city.

When the team returned for a second deployment, from June to November 2004, it found Kandahar a different place. The environment had changed, and violence had significantly increased. The SF teams no longer controlled the battlespace; control was passed to conventional forces that adopted a more threatening posture. The incidence of heavy-handed raids, sweeps, and other combat operations grew. Afghan militias were disbanded without any serious effort to disarm or reintegrate them.

From June to November 2004, the team saw the city of Kandahar backsliding and destabilizing. The team's population-centric focus had been successful the year before, but changes since had created problems that were not easily solved. The Taliban was able to infiltrate back into the city and build a base of support among the population. Violence continued to increase, tensions between U.S. forces and the people grew, and it became increasingly difficult to engage with the population.

Vignette 10
UK-Led Task Force
Musa Qala, Helmand, 2006–2009

In the spring of 2006, the British sent two platoons to Musa Qala to prevent the town from falling to the Taliban. Hundreds of insurgents surrounded the small British position and kept it under constant siege. In October, the British withdrew after brokering a controversial cease-fire with the town's elders.

The cease-fire did not last for long. In January 2007, the Taliban invaded Musa Qala, removed the elders, set up its own government, and turned the town into a sanctuary for insurgents across Helmand—a kind of Afghan Fallujah. The Taliban established *sharia* courts, closed schools, banned television and music, conscripted young men, imposed hefty taxes, and restricted women's rights. Public hangings reminded residents of the consequences of their noncompliance.

The British decided to retake the town with American and Afghan help. They did so only after securing the defection of a mid-level Taliban leader. The British worked with the Afghan government to devise a plan for clearing, holding, and rebuilding the town before combat operations began. The Coalition then surrounded Musa Qala, weakened the insurgents' defenses, and isolated them from the surrounding area. Information operations kept the local population informed so they could stay out of harm's way.

In early December 2007, after months of "influence operations," during which Coalition forces slowly encircled the town, several thousand troops retook Musa Qala, aided by Afghan soldiers nominally in the lead. Named Operation Mar Karardad, it was the largest operation to date in southern Afghanistan. The Taliban's defenses quickly collapsed, and few civilians were harmed.

Coalition forces then set up positions in and around Musa Qala. Within days, most of the population returned. By January 2008, there was a new governor, reconstruction projects had begun, and the British were mentoring a new police force. Problems persisted, however, especially outside the district center, where the Taliban remained active.

Political Preparations

The Coalition waited for an optimal time to retake the district center. A major Taliban defection during the fall of 2007 was the catalyst for action. A moderate Taliban leader, Mullah Abdul Salem, reached out to President Hamid Karzai after growing dissatisfied with the Taliban's use of foreign fighters. President Karzai strongly endorsed Mullah Salem and pushed for political negotiations, which led to meetings that included the British and American ambassadors and the ISAF commander.[1]

While Mullah Salem was not a prominent Taliban figure at the time of his defection,[2] he was an influential Alizai tribal leader in Musa Qala.[3] He indicated that he could engineer a tribal uprising against the Taliban in Musa Qala with the help of the Coalition. As part of the negotiations, the government and Coalition promised him some protection.

Following political negotiations, the Coalition worked with the Afghan government and Afghan National Army (ANA) to plan the operation. The Coalition aimed to use minimal force.

Shaping Operations around Musa Qala

A British brigadier commanded shaping operations—or what he referred to as "influence operations"—with the British army's 52 Infantry Brigade. The operations began months before the launch of Operation Mar Karardad, in which they weakened the Taliban both psychologically and in terms of their defenses. From late August to October 2008, Coalition forces killed a reported 250 insurgents, including high-level Taliban political leaders, around Musa Qala, using raids and airstrikes.[4]

The brigadier planned to encircle the district center and then clear it.[5] In early November, he set the first blocking force against the eastern side of Musa Qala. The British marines also patrolled near Mullah Salem's village to help protect him from assassination. The British brigadier then put another blocking force west and northwest of the town.

Coalition forces closed down Taliban supply routes and isolated the town. Small patrols reminded the Taliban (and residents) that the Coalition had not forgotten about them; however, running battles broke out between Coalition troops and the Taliban. The Taliban also carried out attacks in Sangin and other areas of Helmand Province to relieve pressure on Musa Qala.

To keep the population informed, a British-run radio station broadcast information about their military activities. The British also distributed entertainment banned by the Taliban, such as music and movies. At the end of November, the British notified tribal elders of the impending attack.

In early December, Coalition forces moved in slowly from several directions and probed the Taliban's defenses. Aircraft circled overhead and continued to target Taliban leadership.[6]

On 5–6 December, airplanes dropped leaflets warning of an imminent attack. The leaflets urged the tribal leaders to eject the Taliban themselves and encouraged the population to stay indoors; many fled. The Taliban vowed it would stand and fight with over 2,000 fighters.

Clearing Musa Qala

Operation Mar Karardad began on 7 December 2007 at 1600. Following a round of airstrikes, British, Danish, and Estonian troops, along with U.S. forces, advanced from the south.

Before sunset on 7 December, 400 U.S. paratroopers were inserted by helicopter onto the hills eight miles north of the district center. The Americans were to "surround and beat the Taliban on the outskirts of the town."[7] On 8 December, they captured a cell phone tower on a hill that overlooked the town. Heavy fighting followed for the next few days. The Taliban were well organized and prepared, with weapons caches stashed around the town.

As U.S. troops approached the district center from the north, about 4,000 British soldiers (as well as some Danish and Estonian troops) pushed in from the south to cut off fleeing insurgents.[8] Journalists embedded with these units helped publicize the operation.[9] Heavy aerial bombardment targeted Taliban positions as Coalition forces made their approach.

On the first day, mid-level Musa Qala Taliban commander Mullah Tor Jan was killed, followed by the Taliban deputy governor of Helmand Province, Mullah Faizullah, on 9 December.[10] Many other Taliban commanders fled as their forces began to crumble under pressure.

The insurgents loyal to Mullah Salem—about a third of the Taliban's total force in Musa Qala—refused to fight. However, the tribal uprising that Salem had promised never occurred.

Coalition forces slowly worked their way into the district center, carefully passing through minefields along the way. NATO troops had already secured the perimeter when 1,000 Afghan soldiers entered the town from the south. On 10 December, the Coalition reached the district center. With little resistance remaining, the ANA symbolically raised the Afghan flag in the district center on 12 December.

After six days, the Coalition had killed hundreds of Taliban and many other insurgents had escaped to the mountains to the north. With only 3 Coalition troops killed, another 12 wounded, and 3 civilians reported killed, the operation was largely deemed a success.

Holding Musa Qala

After clearing the town, the Coalition set up outpost positions in and around the district center. One ANA *kandak* (a battalion) was put in charge of holding the town.

ISAF forces created a secure perimeter around the Musa Qala district center. The Coalition's main lines of defense were north and south of town; the Taliban did not have much of a presence to the east and west. ISAF troops also established a base outside the district center to the west. Many smaller observation posts surrounded the district center and were manned by a mix of British troops, ANA, and Afghan National Police (ANP). Patrols outside the town came under constant fire.

These outposts created a small security bubble that made it possible for the British to begin rebuilding the district government and police. The Taliban failed to infiltrate the town again.

The local police force re-formed under the area's previous chief of police, a former militia commander. The police chief's 200 or 300 officers came from Lashkar Gah and Kabul. His deputy estimated that the police chief's former militia comprised 75 percent of his police force.[11]

British (and later U.S. Marine) police training teams trained and mentored the ANP and went with them on patrols.[12] By mid-2009, the Musa Qala ANP was "generally regarded as one of the best in Helmand Province."

While the security situation by the end of 2009 was not ideal and security did not extend much outside the district center, Afghan and Coalition forces continued to hold the town. Low-level violence outside the city persisted, and insurgents had made at least four attempts on Governor Salem's life since he assumed office.

Building Musa Qala

The Coalition developed a stabilization plan long before retaking the town, allowing for its immediate implementation after the battle.[13]

An Afghan raises Afghanistan's national flag in Musa Qala on 12 December 2007. (Photos by Cpl Wayne K. Pitsenberger, U.S. Army)

After the operation ended on 12 December, the Coalition immediately began working with the Afghan government to choose a new governor. Members of the British-led provincial reconstruction team (PRT) helped organize a shura to confirm the selection of a governor. In the meantime, the Afghan Independent Directorate of Local Governance and local officials immediately appointed the Helmand deputy governor (a Musa Qala native) as temporary district administrator for Musa Qala.

After some debate, Mullah Salem was appointed governor on 7 January 2008. While he maintained popular support for the first few months in power, his popularity began to fluctuate as complaints of corruption surfaced and he refused to rein in his private militia.

A British military stabilization support team (MSST)—the first of its kind— arrived on 13 December to assess the damage. There was less destruction than had been anticipated. Most buildings simply needed basic repairs due to neglect. However, larger projects, such as rebuilding the central mosque destroyed during insurgent fighting with the British in 2006, were also needed.

The Afghan Ministry of Rural Rehabilitation and Development took the lead in post conflict reconstruction.[14] According to an early estimate, the combined reconstruction plan for Musa Qala included a $13.8 million joint contribution from the Afghan government, the United Kingdom, and the United States. Although that number was expected to decrease after the MSST's assessment, the Afghan government reportedly promised local Afghans more than $60 million for reconstruction and welfare services. Musa Qala received only a small portion of those funds, largely due to its security situation, corruption, and misappropriated funds.

The British PRT started a Musa Qala district branch for the first time and began projects within a few weeks after the operation. Within months, the PRT helped build a school, health clinic, and roads. The PRT also instituted a cash-for-work public works program, employing up to three residents daily.[15]

Yet problems remained. Projects did not always run as smoothly as planned. Locals sometimes complained that public services were more efficient when the Taliban was in control, and security concerns caused the PRT to abandon the cash-for-work program after insurgents killed three laborers.[16] PRT officers also faced difficulties visiting reconstruction projects outside the district center, where security remained poor.

Despite all the gains made in Musa Qala, the governor remained dissatisfied with the amount of reconstruction work completed. He had overpromised and underdelivered.

Many people in the area were still unemployed by the summer of 2009, and bureaucratic hurdles hindered the reconstruction of the central mosque. As Governor Salem said, "Governments earn trust as a result of their actions."[17] He later continued, "I have promised the people so much, but we have delivered so little, and people will turn on me."[18]

Many locals feared that the Taliban would return. One local elder said, "Everyone knows that the town can be taken, but to keep power there is the key thing. It depends on the skill of the government to make the people trust them. If they are not skillful, then the people will turn to the Taliban."[19]

Conclusion

Operation Mar Karardad was a success due in large part to the effective coordination of political and military operations. Coalition forces established a ring of security that allowed governance to grow and reconstruction to commence. The operations described on this vignette are significant for several reasons.

First, political—not military—actions drove the operation. The Coalition worked out a political deal before the military operation began, assisting with the defection of a Taliban leader who supported the Coalition. Mullah Salem was a respected leader in his tribe and in the region. His militia showed their support of the Coalition by not fighting against them during the operation. His defection also gave legitimacy to the retaking of Musa Qala.

The ANA was involved in the planning and execution of the operation. Even though U.S. and Coalition forces endured most of the fighting, the ANA entered the district center and symbolically reasserted control. The operation was highly publicized as an ANA-led operation. The aim was to strengthen Afghans' confidence in their own forces.

The Coalition was wary of collateral damage during its military campaign to clear the insurgents. Information operations were successful in reaching the local populace; the Coalition broadcast its intentions to the public through radio broadcasts and leaflets. It advertised its military operations so that civilians would have ample time to escape without harm. The population returned within days of the fighting.

The Coalition killed several high-level Taliban commanders, which helped break the insurgents' resistance and caused many fighters to flee.

Afghans helped the Coalition devise a post conflict strategy at the same time as the military operation, which allowed for a smooth transition. By formulating a post operational plan in advance, the Afghan government was able to immediately begin reconstruction projects. A local shura elected a popular local leader, Mullah Salem, who was also endorsed by the central Afghan government.

Finally, the ring of security maintained by the British allowed governance to progress without being subject to direct pressure by the Taliban. Coalition mentors helped stand up and support an ANP force.

Vignette 11
British Marine Battalion
Uruzgan and Helmand, 2008–2009

From September 2008 to April 2009, a reinforced battalion, or battle group, of British marines operated across southern Afghanistan—mostly in remote insurgent base areas. Their activities ranged from brief raids to month-long operations that involved long-range patrols and the construction of fixed bases.

In some operations, the marines did not fire a shot; in others, they fought pitched battles. This vignette describes four missions in the mountains of Uruzgan Province and in the deserts and heavily cultivated areas of southern and central Helmand.

In Uruzgan's IED-laden Mirabad Valley, the marines arrived in strength by helicopter, spoke with tribal leaders, accurately diagnosed the cause of unrest, and devised a political solution that other units later implemented. Roadside bomb attacks then dropped dramatically.

In the "Fishhook" area of southern Helmand, the battle group disrupted a key transit area for foreign fighters and collected information that proved vital during later clear-hold-build operations.

In the lush areas around Marjah and Nad Ali in central Helmand, the battle group fought against hundreds of insurgents in entrenched positions. The marines struck at several insurgent safe areas and established patrol bases under fire, although these bases were later abandoned.

The battle group was a mobile unit based loosely out of Kandahar Airfield, not a "ground-holding force" responsible for a fixed battlespace. It went wherever it was needed—usually to places where there was no Coalition presence and where insurgents operated in strength.

This vignette is based on interviews with officers from 42 Commando, Royal Marines—the battalion commander and his three company commanders—in London on 24 February 2010.

When entering insurgent-controlled areas, the battle group remained constantly on the move. Restraint and local engagement were at the core of every mission to smooth the way for later clear-hold-build operations.

Diagnosing Problems and Proposing Political Solutions in the Mirabad Valley, Uruzgan, October 2008

In mid-October 2008, the battle group entered the Mirabad Valley east of Tarin Kowt, the provincial capital of Uruzgan, to help the province's Dutch-led task force. There were reports of numerous IEDs laid across the valley, which restricted movement through the area. There were no NATO or Afghan forces there.

The 42 Commando battle group flew into the valley and remained for 10 days, during which they moved constantly. Although they did not fire a shot, they did find large quantities of explosives.

By speaking with the valley's elders, the marines learned a great deal about the area's political dynamics. The people of the Mirabad harbored deep—and quite legitimate—grievances against the government and NATO forces. The valley's population came mostly from Ghilzai tribes, which had been shut out of power by Durrani clans that dominated the provincial government in Tarin Kowt.

To reach the provincial capital at Tarin Kowt—to sell their produce or purchase goods in the town's bazaars—the valley's residents had to pass through checkpoints manned by corrupt police who extorted money from travelers. The chief of police had a reputation for kidnapping and raping local boys. NATO forces in Tarin Kowt supported the government, and by extension, the provincial police so despised by the people of the Mirabad.

The Taliban skillfully exploited these grievances to recruit fighters and build a base of support against the government. The insurgents provided weapons, explosives, and military training. Many local people looked to the Taliban for protection against the rapacious police. Allying with the insurgents and laying IEDs was a way to prevent NATO forces from extending the reach of seemingly corrupt and predatory government officials from outside the valley.

After gathering this information, 42 Commando passed it on to Dutch forces, who sacked the police chief and put a stop to extortion at the checkpoints leading into the valley. The Dutch then brought the Ghilzai leaders from the Mirabad into the political process. Soon after the battle group operation, some 70 elders from the Mirabad attended a shura in the provincial capital for the first time. With the elders' permission, the Dutch established a company-sized Afghan National Army outpost three kilometers inside the valley. The elders were also given support to form their own local militia.

Soon after, the Dutch were able to move freely through the Mirabad Valley without fear of IEDs. There were also fewer IED attacks in the provincial capital in Tarin Kowt.

Occupying Insurgent-Controlled Ground Near Marjah and Nad Ali in Central Helmand, December 2008

In December 2008, the battle group participated in a three-week-long brigade-level operation to secure the area around Lashkar Gah, the provincial capital of Helmand. Two

British Marines patrol in Nad Ali District of Helmand Province on 3 January 2009.
(Photo by Cpl John Scott Rafoss, U.S. Marine Corps)

months earlier, several hundred insurgents—most of them based around the Taliban-controlled towns of Marjah and Nad Ali to the south—had nearly overrun Lashkar Gah.

The job of the 42 Commando battle group was to strike at insurgents in Marjah and Nad Ali to keep them off balance while NATO units carried out operations around Lashkar Gah. The marines were then to set up several patrol bases. Other units were to man the positions once the operation was complete. The area was entirely controlled by the insurgents, who operated there in substantial numbers.

On the night of 7 December, the marines air assaulted into a canal on the edge of the desert between Nad Ali and Marjah. 42 Commando's K Company fought its way to a cluster of compounds and established a patrol base near the village of Kosha Kalay. L Company pushed six kilometers southwest to stop insurgents moving north from Marjah. The battalion's company-sized reconnaissance force moved to occupy a position along a canal to the east. The patrol base sat on an important five-way junction between Nawa, Nad Ali, Marjah, and Lashkar Gah.

At both outposts, the insurgents fought pitched battles and beat a tactical retreat. They watched, waited, then split into small groups, surrounded the nascent patrol bases, and hit them with heavy weapons. The insurgents fired and moved at night, which is unusual in Afghanistan, and nearly shot down several helicopters with rocket-propelled grenades (RPGs). For five days, the two companies fought off attacks from all sides while engineers labored to set up fortifications.

The marines counterattacked by pushing small teams out to engage the insurgents. They laid ambushes and maneuvered on the insurgents surrounding the two positions. After nearly a week of fighting, attacks on the bases began to decline.

The marines then pushed patrols farther south toward Marjah. They constantly varied their routes to keep the insurgents from establishing forward lines or identifying patterns. Despite these efforts, the insurgents began employing IEDs, which restricted the battle group's movements out of the two bases.

After more than nine days of heavy fighting, the battle group handed the bases off to another British unit, which stationed a platoon of soldiers in each position—not nearly enough to adequately defend them, much less patrol the surrounding area. The insurgents later encircled the two positions and kept them under constant siege. The bases were subsequently shut down.

Shaping the "Fishhook" in Southern Helmand for Later Clear-Hold-Build Operations, February to March 2009

In February and March 2009, the 42 Commando battle group carried out a month-long operation in an area known as the "Fishhook" in Garmshir District in southern Helmand, near the border with Pakistan. The goal was to gather information and disrupt insurgent movement through the area in preparation for later clear-hold-build operations by U.S. Marines.

The area was a logistical hub and through point for men and material moving between Pakistan and central and northern Helmand. The only operations conducted in the Fishhook since 2001 had been brief raids, none of them lasting longer than 12 hours.

Most of the marines arrived by helicopter, the rest in vehicles. They conducted numerous air and ground assaults from a temporary base in the desert. Some of these were targeted raids against groups of foreign fighters. Others involved extensive patrols and local engagement, which yielded information that the battle group handed over to U.S. Marines planning to set up bases in the area.

In Marjah Again to Dislodge the Taliban, March 2009

In March 2009, the battle group was ordered to leave Garmshir and return to the area between Marjah and Nad Ali in central Helmand for a movement-to-contact operation. The mission was to fly in, engage the enemy, and then leave, in order to keep the insurgents tied down while Coalition units rotated out of the provincial capital.

Insurgents descended on the helicopter landing sites as soon as the marines touched down. The Taliban fired at the helicopters, forcing several to fall back, and fixed the marines with heavy weapons, rockets, and mortars.

Most of the local population fled. With the civilians gone, it became a conventional-style battle. For three days, the marines and the insurgents fought to seize and hold ground. The marines called in bombers, attack helicopters, and artillery. The insurgents took heavy casualties, with some 100 killed. The battle group's three air assault

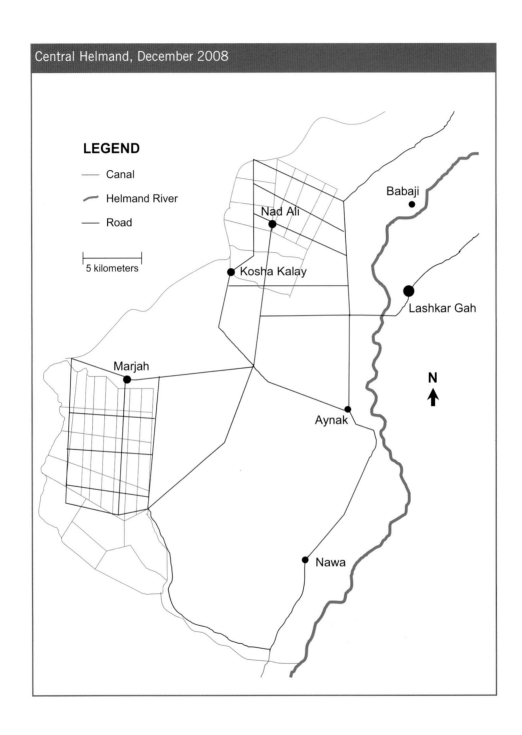

Central Helmand, December 2008

LEGEND

— Canal

⌇ Helmand River

— Road

5 kilometers

Babaji

Nad Ali

Kosha Kalay

Lashkar Gah

Marjah

Aynak

N

Nawa

companies remained under constant fire in different locations. For two days they were tied down and unable to maneuver.

On the third day, the three companies managed to link up and push south toward Marjah where about 200 insurgents were believed to be defending the town from entrenched positions. As the battle group pushed south in staggered formation, the insurgents retreated into the town. On the fourth day, the battle group pushed back north and returned to base.

Conclusion

The 42 Commando battle group was able to create breathing space for other units to operate and collect information for later operations, but its operations were rarely decisive or enduring on their own.

It was up to ground-holding units (those responsible for providing security in a limited area) doing traditional clear-hold-build operations to pacify key areas. When other units were not adequately resourced for the hold phase, the gains made by the battle group did not last—for example, the two patrol bases near Marjah in December 2008 that were later shut down.

For 42 Commando, mobility was essential. The marines' best form of protection was to remain constantly on the move—to take the fight to the Taliban and avoid patterned movements that might make them vulnerable to IEDs and ambushes. As a mobile air assault force, the battle group was able to strike deep into insurgent-controlled territory to keep the enemy off balance and retain some of the initiative.

Ground-holding forces, on the other hand, were fixed by the bases out of which they operated. Patterned movements became unavoidable. Insurgents in Helmand tended to retreat in the face of major clearing operations. They waited, took note of new patrol bases, lines of communication, and repeated movements and then used IEDs and ambushes to restrict the movement of holding forces and limit their access to the population. Marines of 42 Commando learned that after about 36 hours, the advantage of surprise wore off. Insurgents from the surrounding area were then able to pinpoint the marines' location, identify their patterns, maneuver against them, and lay IEDs.

The 42 Commando battle group saw its mission as disrupt, exploit, influence, and understand. The battle group air lifted into remote areas, hoping to exploit the element of surprise to target insurgents and find arms caches. The marines then engaged the population, especially during longer operations. There were rarely plans to leave holding forces behind. The battle group's approach, therefore, was to act as honorably as it could to leave a lasting positive impression. Finally, the marines aimed to learn as much as they could about local conditions and political dynamics, and often passed this information on to units planning future clear-hold-build operations in the area.

The marines learned to pay attention to the political causes of unrest; they found that every area of Afghanistan was its own microcosm of complicated politics and tribal conflict. In the Mirabad Valley, the battle group went in, accurately diagnosed the root causes of violence and resentment against the government, and provided this information to Dutch forces who then remedied the problem—all without firing a shot. There was no need to do clear-hold-build operations once a political solution had been reached.

British Army Advisors
Sangin, Helmand, 2009

From April to October 2009, a company of British army advisors fought to hold the strategic town of Sangin in northern Helmand against insurgents who had infiltrated back into the area. Small teams of 8 to 10 British troops conducted daily foot patrols with their Afghan counterparts from a series of small patrol bases located on the outskirts of town.

The insurgents targeted the patrols relentlessly with improvised explosive devices (IEDs), ambushes, and suicide attacks to deny the soldiers access to the population and keep them away from key transit routes. Sangin in 2009 was one of the most heavily mined areas of Afghanistan and the most dangerous for British troops.

The town was a key poppy producing area and a logistical hub for the insurgents, who enjoyed considerable popular support. Powerful drug barons, who were allied with the Taliban, paid locals to lay IEDs, carry out ambushes, and report on the movements of British and Afghan patrols.

There were believed to be thousands of active IEDs planted in and around the town. The threat dominated everything the soldiers attempted to do and kept them away from many populated areas.

The soldiers found that the most effective countermeasures were regular foot patrols and engagement with the population. Yet patrols moved slowly. Forced to search constantly for IEDs in the soft ground of footpaths and mud walls, they were barely able to move 1,500 meters in a day.

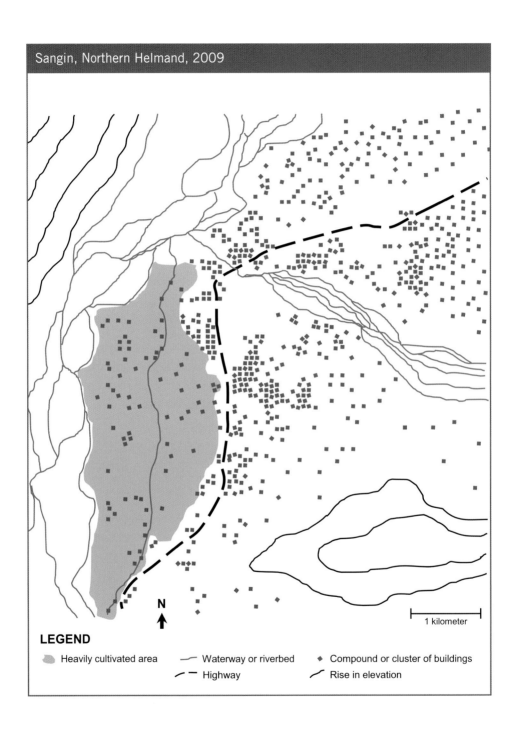

Sangin, Northern Helmand, 2009

LEGEND

- Heavily cultivated area
- Highway
- Waterway or riverbed
- Rise in elevation
- Compound or cluster of buildings

N

1 kilometer

Outposting Sangin

The British army advisors, from 1st Battalion Welsh Guards, were part of an Operational Mentoring and Liaison Team (OMLT) responsible for training and advising a 400-man battalion of Afghan soldiers spread around Sangin. The team had 45 troops, most of them noncommissioned officers, operating out of four patrol bases within three kilometers of the district center.

Advising the Afghan army in Sangin was dangerous work. Small teams patrolled alongside Afghan soldiers without much of the support and enablers available to dedicated combat forces. They moved on foot out of fixed bases with IEDs along nearly every possible patrol route.

A reinforced battalion, or battle group, of British soldiers from 2 Rifles served as the area's ground-holding force. They were based near the district center and bazaar, and spread across a number of satellite positions in Sangin and points north.

Sangin was a hotly contested area. Intense fighting in 2006 had forced much of the population to flee. Security improved in 2008 with more troops, patrols, and outposts. Many people returned and shops reopened. Yet the Taliban and drug traffickers returned as well, with more sophisticated tactics. Insurgents wielded considerable influence and moved freely, even in areas that were regularly patrolled.

Many soldiers in Sangin were convinced that much of the population was behind the insurgents and the drug barons who paid the locals to fight and lay IEDs. Most fighters were landless laborers who worked in the poppy fields during the growing season and fought for money when the harvest was over. Many locals provided tips on IEDs, but they also kept the Taliban informed about the movements of British and Afghan patrols.

IEDs and the Struggle for Access to the Population

The IED threat in Sangin was monumental—greater than anywhere else in Afghanistan. For example, an estimated 1,200 IEDs were planted in the cultivated areas south of the Sangin district center—an area that is just one square kilometer. There were also at least that many planted inside the town itself and to the north and east.

The IED cells operating in Sangin were sophisticated, ruthless, and persistent. The insurgents planted bombs indiscriminately in large numbers along every possible patrol route and around every patrol base (often within 30 meters of the base walls) and detonated them by remote control or command wire.

In just six months, from April to October 2009, 22 British soldiers were killed in Sangin, most of them in IED explosions while on foot patrol. In 2009, 2 Rifles experienced one of the highest casualty rates of any U.S. or British battalion in Afghanistan since the beginning of the war in 2001. Sangin, a town of less than 20,000 people in 2009, accounts for over one-third of British casualties in Afghanistan.[1]

The 2 Rifles battle group took most of its casualties in the urban areas near the district center. The area was marked by a maze of alleyways and canalizations between closely built compounds. The routes through were predictable and bombs were easy to plant and hide.[2]

The insurgents used explosive devices to restrict the movement of British and Afghan troops and to deny them access to the population. The IED problem was so extreme that counter-IED operations became, in effect, the primary activity of British advisors while on foot patrol. The advisors found IEDs almost every day, many of them low-metal content devices that were very difficult to detect. Insurgents laid IEDs around British reconstruction projects, such as wells and bridges.

The advisors were forced to move at a snail's pace, constantly sweeping the ground for bombs, diffusing the devices, and disposing of them. As a result, the advisors were not able to regularly patrol more than 1.5 kilometers beyond their bases. The areas of persistent presence around each of the four patrol bases barely touched. Much of the cultivated area south of the district center was under de facto Taliban control.

Some of the most dangerous missions the advisors undertook were resupply convoys between the district center and outlying patrol bases. The insurgents laid IEDs in large numbers along all motorable roads. The Taliban were able to predict the routes and frequency of most resupply convoys, despite the soldiers' best efforts to avoid setting patterns. The advisors lost three Afghan soldiers during resupply missions.

The Welsh Guards found that the best countermeasure was regular foot patrols. The more the soldiers spoke with locals and built trust around their patrol bases, the more information came in about IED locations. Regular patrolling—and the constant fighting and risk of IED explosions that went along with it—were essential to keeping the insurgents away from the base and the villages nearby, and securing the cooperation of the locals.

Shifting Front Lines

If the advisors reduced the tempo of their patrols in any way, the insurgents immediately took advantage by pushing closer to the bases. There were clearly identifiable front lines—what the British called "forward lines of enemy troops," or FLETs—that the insurgents heavily mined and fiercely defended. The insurgents pushed constantly to move their defensive lines (and hence the ground they effectively controlled) closer to the patrol bases. For the advisors, holding Sangin was a constant struggle to hold their ground and push these lines back. Progress was measured in tens or hundreds of meters.

With the end of the poppy harvest in June, the insurgents stepped up their tempo of operations and pushed steadily closer to the four patrol bases. There were attacks every day on all four positions; many of these attacks were quite sophisticated. By August, patrols were not able to walk more than 200 meters in any direction without hitting a wall of IEDs and heavy small-arms and RPG fire.

The advisors struggled to keep the roads open for resupply between their patrol bases and the battalion headquarters at the district center. It became increasingly difficult for the advisors to persuade Afghan soldiers to patrol beyond their bases. Fewer and fewer local people showed up for shuras and contact with the population diminished considerably.

Conclusion

IEDs in extraordinary numbers stood between British troops and the population of Sangin. Soldiers on foot were forced to move extremely slowly, greatly reducing the areas that could be regularly patrolled. Insurgents used IEDs to keep Coalition forces out of certain areas and away from the population. Projecting influence into these areas was a constant struggle involving considerable risk.

There were no easy answers to the problem. Regular foot patrols and interaction with the population—the very activities that insurgents used IEDs to restrict and prevent—proved to be the best countermeasure against homemade bombs. Counterinsurgency and counter-IED operations went hand in hand; both required ease of movement and access to the population.

Insurgents operated underground in substantial numbers. This presented considerable challenges to British and Afghan troops. The Coalition had cleared Sangin in 2007 and held it with a substantial force dispersed across small outposts—just what counterinsurgency doctrine recommends. Despite these efforts, the insurgents infiltrated back in again in 2008. Even with an entire battalion of British and Afghan troops, it was a constant struggle to control even small pieces of territory. IED blasts were a persistent occurrence, even in areas that were regularly patrolled.

The measure of influence that Coalition forces enjoyed in Sangin could be determined in large part by the area they were able to regularly patrol. The extent of this area shifted with the tempo of operations on either side of the conflict. From April to June 2009, the ground patrolled by British forces included most of Sangin and its outlying areas. But from late June to October, the insurgents stepped up their attacks, pushing the front lines, so to speak, to within 200 meters of most patrol bases and retaking much of the town. British forces later pushed back with intensified operations and more patrol bases.

Economics drove the tempo of operations on the enemy side. During the poppy season, which lasted until June, most men able and inclined to fight were gainfully employed in the opium harvest. From late June on, the Taliban and drug barons paid these men to fight and lay IEDs. For this reason alone, it can be said that much of the population of Sangin was behind the insurgency—not because British and Afghan forces were not doing counterinsurgency the right way, but because there was plenty of money to be made by fighting.

Vignette 13
Two Dutch Army Companies
Uruzgan, 2006–2009

Beginning in the summer of 2006, Dutch battle groups based in Tarin Kowt, the provincial capital of Uruzgan, began pushing companies into remote valleys to the north and west. The soldiers operated far from reinforcements in areas where the Taliban had freedom of movement.

Despite a long history of Taliban influence, local populations proved surprisingly cooperative. In many areas, the Dutch were able to build a solid base of popular support.

This vignette focuses on operations in two locations: Deh Rawood, a large valley surrounded by mountains 40 kilometers west of Tarin Kowt; and Chora and the Baluchi Valley, a remote string of villages 30 kilometers north of the provincial capital. It covers Dutch operations in Deh Rawood from July to December 2006 and November 2008 to April 2009, and in Chora and the Baluchi Valley from November 2008 to April 2009.

Deh Rawood, July to December 2006

In July 2006, the Dutch sent a company of soldiers to Deh Rawood. Surrounded by mountains on all sides, the area was totally isolated from the outside world. Mullah Omar, the Taliban's top leader, had lived in Deh Rawood as a child. Much of the local population knew nothing about the U.S. invasion and the ouster of the Taliban. When they saw the Dutch, many people believed the Russians had returned.

The soldiers operated almost entirely on their own, as a mountain range separated them from their higher headquarters in Tarin Kowt. The soldiers conducted regular foot patrols—often lasting several days—and stretching as far as 10 kilometers from the firebase. Many patrols involved driving to outlying areas, setting up a base camp, and hiking seven to eight kilometers to far-flung villages accessible only on foot. According to

---

Unless otherwise noted, this vignette is based on interviews with Dutch army officers at the Royal Military Academy in Breda, the Netherlands, on 1 March 2010.

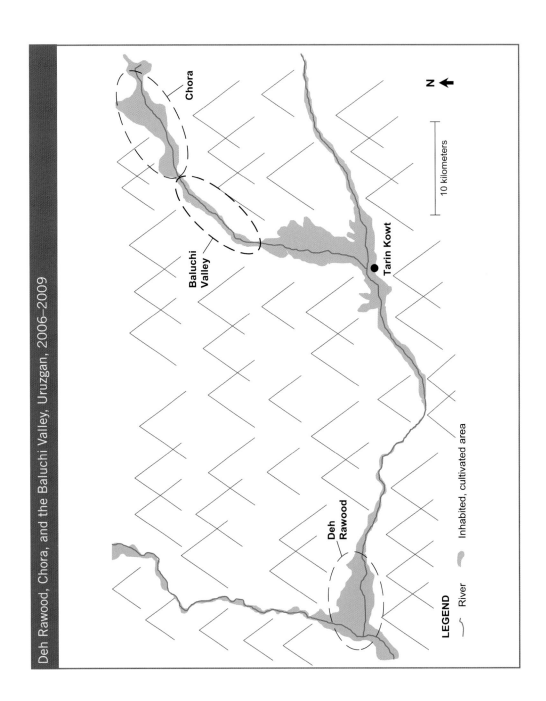

Deh Rawood, Chora, and the Baluchi Valley, Uruzgan, 2006–2009

Chora

Baluchi
Valley

Tarin Kowt

Deh
Rawood

N

10 kilometers

LEGEND

River   Inhabited, cultivated area

one of the platoon commanders, these multiday foot patrols were the only way to reach remote villages and exert substantial influence in the valley. Village leaders sometimes warned the soldiers about ambushes on their way back to base. Yet these rarely occurred; there were few attacks on the Dutch in Deh Rawood in 2006.

Over time, the soldiers began to understand the rudiments of the tribal dynamic in the areas they patrolled. They learned that there were long-standing rivalries among different villages and clans. Village leaders often spoke ill of elders in nearby hamlets. These local power brokers often accused their rivals of working for the Taliban. The Dutch suspected that many of these claims were false, and that rival factions were manipulating the Coalition's campaign against the Taliban to gain an advantage in local disputes.

For example, in one area of the valley, two rival power brokers, both strongmen from different tribes, lived close together and had tribal militias who occasionally fired on Dutch troops. The two had a long history of conflict, much of it over land they both claimed. One of these power brokers, who had been close to U.S. forces during the early years of the war, repeatedly accused the other of working for the Taliban, prompting raids and arrests by U.S. forces.

It was never clear to the Dutch whether (or to what extent) these accusations were true. It was apparent, however, that the Taliban exploited local rivalries, siding with local power brokers who were out of favor with the government or Coalition. U.S. forces in the area tended to ally with certain local strongmen, often not realizing that by doing so they were taking sides in local disputes, thereby earning the enmity of rival clans and creating opportunities that the Taliban easily exploited. The Dutch were keen to avoid taking sides.

The Dutch understood that maintaining neutrality in local disputes was essential. With this in mind, Dutch forces treated the human intelligence they received with considerable skepticism. The soldiers also learned the importance of visiting leaders from both sides involved in ongoing disputes or rivalries and spreading reconstruction money around as much as possible.

Deh Rawood, November 2008 to April 2009

By November 2008, the Dutch had built four bases in Deh Rawood: a large forward operating base and three small patrol bases. A small Dutch army company of three platoons operated out of these positions. The soldiers shared the area with several Afghan army companies and their advisors, a team of French soldiers.

Since the Dutch forces' arrival in Deh Rawood in July 2006, the Taliban had grown in strength, quietly infiltrating back into the valley in late 2007. They came in small groups, rented houses, and befriended locals with gifts and money. They then went on the offensive, destroying bridges built by the Coalition, targeting locals believed to be collaborating with the Dutch, and overrunning police checkpoints.

The Dutch launched a series of operations against the resurgent Taliban, forcing the insurgents into the hills and the outskirts of the valley. The Dutch also stepped up foot patrols and invested more money in reconstruction. These operations met with substantial popular support. By the fall of 2008, Deh Rawood was stable, though Taliban influence remained strong beyond the fringes of Dutch control. The insurgents chose not to fight for the valley, and the Dutch did not pursue them into their mountain redoubts.

After pushing the Taliban back, the Dutch soldiers conducted daily foot patrols through the valley, many of them with Afghan troops. Many of these patrols lasted for three to four days and involved staying overnight in far-flung areas of the valley. The Dutch found that after they visited remote villages a few times, people began to open up and cooperate.

There were no major attacks on Dutch forces in the valley in the fall of 2008 and the spring of 2009. Locals turned in IEDs and provided actionable intelligence on impending suicide attacks. In February 2009, the Taliban tried to organize a suicide attack to assassinate the district police chief. The Dutch heard about the plan and—along with U.S., French, and Afghan forces—raided the village where the bomber had taken refuge.

Chora and the Baluchi Valley, November 2008 to April 2009

In Chora District, 30 kilometers north of Tarin Kowt, the story was similar to Deh Rawood. In 2007, the Dutch had successfully forced the Taliban out of the area and kept them out with the help of local tribal leaders. Many people from outlying areas built houses near Dutch bases, hoping to benefit from the security bubble created by the soldiers' presence. There were few major attacks on Dutch patrols in Chora in 2008 and none in 2009.

The Dutch focused on daily foot patrols, going as far as five kilometers from their bases (within reach of their 81mm mortars) and meeting and talking to farmers and local leaders, most of whom were easily accessible and willing to talk to the soldiers. The Dutch also conducted mounted patrols to reach the more distant villages. Within this radius of regular foot patrols, locals in any given area saw the Dutch about once every five days; those closer to the base interacted on a daily basis.

The Dutch rarely carried out raids or other combat operations where they regularly patrolled, in part because doing so was unnecessary, and in part because the soldiers were extremely careful not to do anything that might jeopardize the relationships they had built.

The company held regular shuras with village and tribal leaders to decide on small-scale reconstruction projects done through local contractors. Civilians and soldiers from the Dutch provincial reconstruction team handled most of these meetings. It took multiple shuras before the Dutch were able to achieve consensus on how reconstruction funds should be spent. The soldiers allowed the district governor to mediate disputes among elders over projects, which gave him considerable power.

Beyond the radius of regular patrols, Dutch soldiers relied almost entirely on local tribal leaders to deny insurgent influence. Some of these leaders fought off the Taliban; others cut deals with the insurgents. In much of Chora, there were identifiable leaders—most of them pro government Barakzai tribesmen who had allied with the Dutch.

Where local allies were not available or where tribal leaders were sympathetic to the Taliban, the insurgents managed to infiltrate the villages and exert substantial influence. This was the case in the Baluchi Valley to the southwest, where militants constantly attacked Dutch forces. The area was a thicket of competing Hotaki and Tokhi Ghilzai clans that had no discernible leadership with which to engage. The only power broker that the Dutch knew of in the valley was a former district governor, but he was killed in a raid sometime in the early fall of 2008. The man's son had assumed his father's mantle but was known as a weak figure who was susceptible to Taliban influence.

Dutch, British, and Australian forces had swept through the valley in 2006 and 2007, carrying out raids and attempting to clear it of insurgents but leaving no forces behind to hold the area or engage with its population. The insurgents returned after each of these operations.

In mid-January 2008, the Dutch carried out a relatively large operation to clear and hold the Baluchi Valley where about 150 to 200 enemy fighters were believed to be operating. The soldiers cleared through the valley, searching about 400 compounds. They patrolled the valley constantly for the rest of January and all of February and set up a patrol base, manned by two platoons, in late February. The Dutch then started small-scale reconstruction projects and tried to identify cooperative leaders through a shura involving 40 to 50 people. After about six weeks, the Dutch began to see growing cooperation, especially tips on IEDs. Yet in the spring of 2009, insurgents began trickling back into the valley, carrying out attacks.

The expansion into the restive Baluchi Valley had forced the Dutch to take forces out of Chora, endangering many of the gains made there. The Dutch company was ordered to send one of its two available rifle platoons to the valley, cutting patrols in Chora by nearly half. The soldiers were no longer able to maintain the level of interaction with the populace they had before, causing many of the relationships they had built to fray.

Conclusion

Deh Rawood, Chora, and the Baluchi Valley are extremely remote areas effectively cut off from the outside world. Dutch soldiers learned to relate to a local population that was almost entirely illiterate and to be patient and focus on cultivating personal relationships based on trust. They also learned the importance of understanding local tribal dynamics and finding and engaging local leaders. Over time, the Dutch managed to build a solid base of support in what had been a Taliban safe haven.

The soldiers did so by remaining neutral in local disputes and treating the intelligence they received with skepticism. Past raids based on faulty information had pushed many local leaders into the Taliban camp and alienated entire communities.

The Dutch followed an oil-spot strategy that involved focusing on small areas where they could make a difference, recognizing that the Taliban would continue to operate farther afield. This strategy put considerable constraints on the Dutch military's capacity to expand into new areas. The Taliban was able to operate beyond the fringes of Dutch control, but Dutch influence remained strong in the areas where its forces were concentrated.

By late 2008, the Dutch had reached the point at which going into new areas required thinning out troops in other places where they were still needed. They faced a dilemma common to many counterinsurgency forces: the more areas they cleared and held, the more thinly spread their forces became and the fewer forces they had in each place, making them less effective and less secure. Rather than expand farther, the Dutch focused on the areas they already controlled. In the words of one Dutch army company commander, "The problem is that when you have a static number of troops, you become the victim of your own success when you expand."

Dutch Marine Company
Deh Rashaan, Uruzgan, 2009

From July to December 2009, a company of Dutch marines built a network of support-ers in the insurgent-controlled Deh Rashaan Valley in Uruzgan Province without actually establishing a permanent presence. Deh Rashaan is about 10 to 15 kilometers north of Tarin Kowt, the provincial capital and the headquarters of the Dutch-led Task Force Uruzgan.

The marines launched regular, multiday missions into the valley in an attempt to gain a foothold in the area. The company patrolled on foot throughout the valley, mostly at night, forming alliances with local leaders and recruiting local militiamen to guide them into the more dangerous areas of the valley. The marines moved around constantly and operated from mobile patrol bases, never using the same site twice.

These regular "shaping" operations later allowed the Dutch to establish permanent bases manned by Afghan police without facing much resistance. The relationships they had formed and the information they had gathered proved essential to influencing the area in 2010.

Mobile Patrol Bases, Foot Patrols at Night

The mission of the Dutch marines was to project influence into Deh Rashaan, gather useful information, and find leaders to work with. They accomplished this through con-tinuous, small-scale, multiday missions.

The marines pushed into the valley periodically for seven to 10 days at a time. They raided suspected insurgent compounds, met with village leaders, and talked to local people. A typical mission involved driving into the valley, circling the vehicles as a makeshift base, and then patrolling the villages by foot.

This vignette is based on an interview with a Dutch Marine company commander attached to the Dutch-led Task Force Uruzgan from July to December 2009. Interview conducted at the Royal Military Academy in Breda, the Netherlands, on 1 March 2010.

Dutch Marines on patrol in the Deh Rashaan Valley. (Photo by Royal Netherlands Marine Corps)

The marines moved on foot during the night and often slept in local compounds during the day. Sleeping in the villages allowed them to patrol deep into the valley without having to return to their makeshift base after every night patrol. Rather than rent a compound, which would have left its owner open to accusations of collaborating with the Coalition, the Dutch usually slept in buildings where they found weapons, which provided them some justification for seizing the building temporarily. They also drank local water, rather than carrying water with them, which allowed them more freedom of movement.

The marines established makeshift patrol bases in different locations every time and avoided using the same route twice or sleeping in the same compound. They believed that operating from fixed bases would establish predictable patrol patterns, such as moving to and from the same base every day, making them vulnerable to attacks.

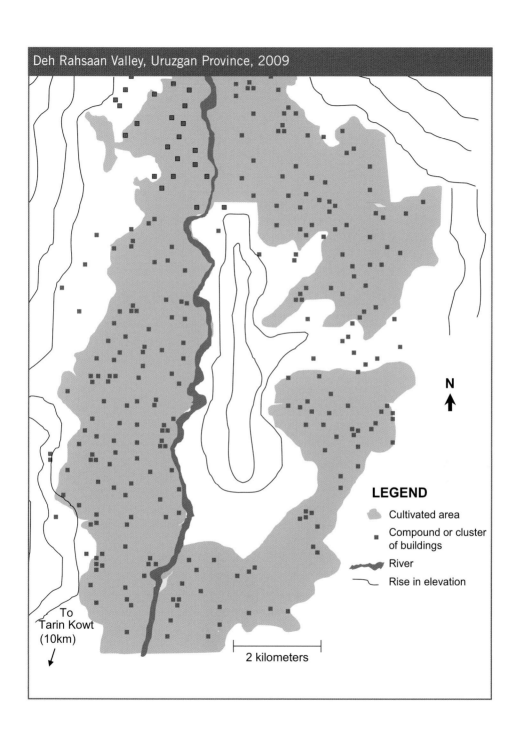

Deh Rahsaan Valley, Uruzgan Province, 2009

N

LEGEND

Cultivated area

Compound or cluster of buildings

River

Rise in elevation

To Tarin Kowt (10km)

2 kilometers

There were relatively few direct-fire attacks in Deh Rashaan; the main threat was IEDs. After the marines launched several week-long operations into the valley, the insurgents started laying IEDs all over the valley, anywhere the troops were likely to go on foot. The insurgents' aim was to limit the mobility of the foot patrols and deny them access to the population, by forcing them to creep along at a snail's pace, always on the lookout for explosives.

Local people were more willing to talk to the marines at night. The insurgents mostly operated during the day, as did their informants in the villages. The patrols' most productive times were just after dusk and shortly before first light, when people were out but it was still quite dark. Local elders sought out the marines during these times.

In early 2010, shortly after the marines returned to the Netherlands, the remaining Dutch forces established two police outposts in the Deh Rashaan Valley. The effort to set up the outposts met with little resistance, largely due to the shaping operations by the Dutch marine company. The outpost facilitated the construction of a road from Tarin Kowt north to Chora, a valley beyond Deh Rashaan where the Dutch operated several small bases.

Local Guides, Local Politics

Deh Rashaan was divided between two main groups: Ghilzai tribes in the northern part of the valley, most of whom were hostile to the government and sympathetic to the Taliban, and the Popalzai and other non-Ghilzai groups to the south, who were more supportive of Coalition forces. If locals were unwilling to talk to the marines, the patrol moved on and did not return, figuring it was better to focus on people who showed some desire to cooperate.

The marines acquired the most influence in the Popalzai areas; from there, the company pushed north. After several months of operations, the Dutch developed sources in some Ghilzai villages. Many who cooperated were active or former Taliban, usually with some interest to serve. Ghilzai elders told the marines that Australian and American forces had killed civilians in artillery and air strikes, causing many to take up arms against the Coalition. Though willing to talk to the marines, these elders were open about their support to the insurgents and were not willing to establish a serious working relationship with the Coalition.

When patrolling into the Ghilzai areas, the marines often used local guides recruited from non-Ghilzai villages in the southern part of the valley. These guides knew the terrain and the people. Some were members of a local Popalzai militia whose commander offered to cooperate with the marines after the Taliban reportedly killed his son. These local militiamen showed the marines ambush positions, IED sites, and insurgent transit routes. A patrol that might take the marines six hours on their own took only one hour with the help of local guides. The guides refused to operate during the day but were not afraid to move into Ghilzai areas at night.

Despite their obvious value, the company learned that these local militiamen could not be completely trusted. They came from nearby non-Ghilzai villages, and many of them had an axe to grind against the Ghilzais. The guides often tried to manipulate the marine company to serve their own local interests or those of their leaders. The valley's Popalzai villages had many disputes with the Ghilzais. Popalzai leaders tried to use the marines against their rivals to the north, just as the Ghilzais used the Taliban against the Popalzai.

The marines tried to avoid getting involved in these disputes, but neutrality was not always possible. The simple fact that the marines were allied with the government—and therefore were associated with its officials, allies, tribal affiliations, and all it represented—sometimes forced them to take sides.

Conclusion

The marine company learned how to work with local militias to navigate the terrain, identify insurgent safe houses, and avoid IEDs. Still, the marines understood enough about local politics to realize that their guides had interests of their own and so could not be completely trusted. Local militiamen proved extremely effective tactically, but taking their side against the restive Ghilzai clans threatened to further inflame the valley's conflicts and strengthen the Taliban politically.

The marines came to understand that the fighting in Deh Rashaan had little to do with the Taliban writ large and everything to do with local politics. Most of the fighters were locals who had received some weapons and training from outsiders. Ongoing feuds between Ghilzai and Popalzai clans mirrored the fighting between insurgents and

Coalition forces. Rival factions formed alliances with outside forces to help them in their local disputes. Even among the Ghilzais, some feuds erupted in bloodshed.

Deh Rashaan was a contested area. Many local people played both sides, cooperating with the marines when it was dark and the insurgents when it was light.

The marines recognized this reality; they did not expect people to side overtly with the Coalition, especially when there was no permanent force in the area to protect them.

The company's practice of pushing into the valley for seven to 10 days at a time to conduct small-scale dismounted patrols—as opposed to doing large-scale clearing operations—allowed the Dutch to project influence north without establishing a permanent presence. These operations were particularly effective at setting the groundwork for later clear-hold-build operations.

By patrolling at night and sleeping in compounds during the day, the marines were able to move freely through Taliban-controlled villages and build a network of supporters. Their use of mobile patrol bases instead of fixed positions allowed them to keep the insurgents off balance and avoid IEDs.

The Dutch marines learned that it was important to vary their activities, such as moving along different routes, talking to different people, or using different tactics. The insurgents were particularly skilled at identifying patterns and adapting quickly, so the marines had to avoid any tendency to fall into habits.

Canadian Soldiers and Engineers
Dand, Kandahar, 2009

From April to November 2009, a company of Canadian soldiers and engineers created an island of peace and stability in the restive Panjwayi Valley south of Kandahar City.

The team initially focused on the village of Deh-e-Bagh in Dand District, then oil-spotted outward into nearby hamlets. Soldiers dispersed into small patrol bases and conducted regular patrols, while engineers implemented projects through local leaders.

The Canadians aimed to employ as many local fighting-age males as possible on low-technology, labor-intensive projects. The engineers spread these jobs out as widely as possible by hiring roughly one person from each compound or extended family.

By the fall of 2009, the insurgents were unable to operate in much of Dand District. Taliban commanders complained they were unable to recruit local fighters. Large-scale job creation effectively tied the local population to the Canadian effort.

Operation Kalay I: April to August 2009

In April 2009, the commander of Canadian forces in Kandahar sent a company of soldiers to the village of Deh-e-Bagh, the administrative center of Dand District, south of Kandahar City. The move was dubbed Operation Kalay I.

The company consisted of a headquarters element, a rifle platoon, civil affairs officers, a psychological operations team, and some diplomatic personnel whose job was to engage with district officials. The company worked alongside a unit of Canadian army engineers known as the Construction Management Organization, which focused on relatively large, low-technology, labor-intensive projects.

This vignette is based on interviews with the 2009 commanders of Stabilization Company B and a 22-man engineer detachment known as the Construction Management Organization—both part of Task Force Kandahar. Interviews conducted on 15 and 26 March 2010.

Afghan Uniformed Police and Canadian soldiers supervise the distribution of food and other aid items. (Photo by Sgt Erich F. Braün)

The hope was that this combined force would be more sensitive to political and economic issues than other combat units and more mission-oriented than provincial reconstruction teams and development agencies manned by civilians.

The company's mission was to go into Deh-e-Bagh, clear out the insurgents, live there, and provide enough security for the district government to get back on its feet and for engineers to employ local people on reconstruction projects. The company would then gradually expand its area of operations as conditions permitted.

In April, the company made several trips to Deh-e-Bagh to gather information and secure the support of the village elders, nearly all of whom were from the same tribe, the Barakzai. One man owned nearly all the area's arable land, which most of the population farmed as sharecroppers. This man gave his support as well.

There was little inherent support for the Taliban in Deh-e-Bagh, although fighters frequently passed through. There were perhaps 20 hardcore insurgents in the area. The rest were part-time fighters, many of whom were in it for the money or because they had little else to do.

On 19 May, Canadian forces went into Deh-e-Bagh. They fanned out across the village and its surroundings without firing a shot. The company set up its patrol base in the village.

On 24 May, with its patrol base secured, the company's civil affairs officers began handing out food, blankets, fuel, and clothing. Two days later, engineers began work on a canal project. They also renovated the district center, paved the central street through the town, and began paving a road to a nomadic camp south of the village. The idea was to immediately link a critical mass of the population to the stabilization effort before the insurgents had time to regroup and infiltrate back into the area.

The engineers' goal was to employ as many local people as possible for as long as possible. To this end, Canadian forces focused on low-technology, labor-intensive projects that took months to complete. By July 2009, there were 340 locals working on various projects in and around Deh-e-Bagh.

The purpose of this operation was to give gainful employment to landless laborers with few marketable skills—those who had joined the Taliban for money and laid most of the

IEDs—and tie them into the Canadian effort. By employing large numbers of fighting-age males, Canadian forces drained much of the Taliban's potential recruiting pool.

The workers received 400 Afghanis per day, based on an estimate of the standard market rate for local labor. The reason for this amount was to pay them more than they might receive from the Taliban, but not enough to cause undue inflation or draw skilled people such as doctors and teachers away from their jobs.

By July, the approach was clearly working. Canadian forces intercepted reports that the insurgents were unable to recruit local fighters in the area around Deh-e-Bagh. Some Taliban commanders reportedly ordered their subordinates not to attack Canadian forces in Deh-e-Bagh, since the soldiers were helping people and doing no harm. By July, attacks on Canadian troops were few and far between.

The Canadians spread jobs evenly across the community and tied each household into the reconstruction effort. Engineers hired roughly one fighting-age male per compound or household. This worked out to about 10 percent of the population. Within a few months, nearly every person in and around Deh-e-Bagh had a close friend or relative working on a Canadian-funded project.

The idea was to avoid giving a disproportionate share of jobs to one clan or faction, for fear of causing resentment among those who felt left out. Such resentment had led to attacks on Canadian projects elsewhere in Kandahar.

To this end, Canadian forces paid the workers directly, rather than through intermediaries. The engineers had learned that giving money to local leaders and relying on them to pay wages to laborers created local power brokers who tended to use their influence to enrich themselves and their fellow clansmen, often at the expense of rival factions.

Canadian engineers avoided hiring anyone from outside the area after learning the hard way that doing so could cause serious problems. For example, a civilian contractor working with Canadian engineers in nearby Panjwayi District hired Pakistani subcontractors for a large road project around the same time as the Deh-e-Bagh operations. Local men issued death threats against the Pakistani subcontractors, accusing them of taking jobs away from locals. Insurgents hit the Pakistanis with IEDs and small arms, and eventually forced them to leave. In the village of Temuryan, south of Deh-e-Bagh, elders

Residents of Deh-e-Bagh work on the renovation of the Dand District Centre. (Photo by Cpl Jonathan Barrette)

threatened to kill a team of stonemasons that the engineers had brought in from Kandahar City. When the Canadians offered to pair local youth with the stonemasons as apprentices, the threats stopped.

Rather than rely on outside contractors, engineers hired and mentored locals with leadership potential and made them leaders of 15-man work teams. The company had a

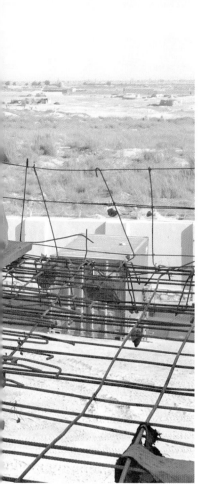

team working on roads, one digging irrigation canals, and another filling in craters. Over time, these teams required less and less supervision. By October 2009, most projects required little Canadian oversight. The engineers visited the projects daily to monitor progress but were no longer involved in day-to-day management.

Deh-e-Bagh was a small place with a relatively homogenous population, most of it from a handful of Barakzai clans. The workers knew each other and were quick to spot outsiders who might be working for the Taliban. By breaking the workers up into small teams led by reliable Afghan partners, the Canadian company was able to prevent the Taliban from infiltrating the work crews as it had done in other areas of Kandahar—for example, in nearby Panjwayi District where rival tribes lived in close proximity and migrant labor was prevalent.

In addition to facilitating reconstruction projects, Canadian soldiers patrolled on foot constantly and met regularly with local leaders. A team of diplomats maintained regular liaison with district officials. Canadian advisors trained the Afghan police and took them on patrols. When conducting searches or raids against suspected insurgents, the soldiers brought a local leader with them to talk to the villagers before the search began.

Canadian troops also worked with local religious leaders, which was unusual for Coalition forces in Afghanistan. The Deh-e-Bagh area had about 12 mosques and two mullahs who tended to preach against the Coalition. After the soldiers decided to refurbish the village's mosques, the mullahs began preaching in support of the Canadian operations.

The company spent many hours talking to local leaders, drinking tea and talking informally about any topic that happened to come up before discussing business matters.

The goal was to build personal relationships and trust. Local leaders began asking the company commander to help resolve disputes and deal with other local issues.

From May through July, Canadian forces focused entirely on a 10-square-kilometer area in and around Deh-e-Bagh. Their goal was to slowly build up Deh-e-Bagh first and allow time for neighboring villages to see the progress being made there.

Before long, elders from nearby villages began asking for projects. Canadian troops called this the "village pull" effect. Even as their resources spread thin, Canadian engineers were reluctant to say no, for fear of inciting resentment among the villages that were denied reconstruction funds.

Operation Kalay II: August to November 2009

Near the end of July, the Canadians decided to expand into villages south and west of Deh-e-Bagh. In August, they set up patrol bases in the villages of Rumbasi, Temuryan, and Belanday—each about five to six kilometers from Deh-e-Bagh (see map). Canadian forces also set up small outposts and reconstruction projects in the villages of Walakan, Anguryan, and Zor Mashor.

In Rumbasi and Temuryan, soldiers first spoke to the mullahs and village elders to gain their consent, and then moved in, set up patrol bases, and began implementing projects. Canadian engineers consulted with village leaders to find a reliable local contractor, who then hired his own security.

In Belanday, near the border with the restive Panjwayi District, the soldiers could not find any local leaders to work with. The village was heavily influenced by Noorzai tribesmen to the west who were adamantly opposed to the Coalition presence. The Canadians went in anyway. They brought their own security for the work crews and managed reconstruction projects directly. There were more attacks in Belanday than in any other part of Dand District, yet the level of violence gradually decreased and local participation grew.

Insurgents targeted the new patrol bases at first, but conditions improved over time. Locals provided information about the insurgents, which Canadian troops used to carry out a series of successful raids that pushed the Taliban farther south and west.

There continued to be isolated attacks, but few attributed to the Taliban. Most were traced to drug traffickers (usually of hashish, not poppy) who were trying to keep Canadian forces away from trafficking routes. By the fall, Dand District had become so stable that the isolated attacks had little effect on local conditions.

By October 2009, almost 700 local people were working on projects in seven villages in Dand District. During that year, the number of locals employed on Canadian projects had increased from 199 in June, to 340 in July, to 434 in August, to 612 in September, and to 689 by October. In November, the number of employed workers was over 1,000.

Oil spotting strained the company of Canadian soldiers as it became increasingly spread out. By August, most outposts had only a section of soldiers, or 10 men—the smallest unit allowed to operate independently in the Canadian army (the company had only 65 fighting troops; the rest were engaged in noncombat related duties).

The soldiers tried to compensate by relying more on the police as a holding force. The problem was that most villagers hated the police. Most of the force was from northern Afghanistan and did not speak Pashtu. Over time, however, Canadian trainers were able to build the police into a reliable and cooperative force that was welcome in much of the area, and even praised by some village leaders. Over time, these police were securing areas on their own, allowing Canadian soldiers to focus their energies elsewhere.

Four different local security forces operated in Dand District. One was the standard Afghan National Police, part of the Ministry of Interior. The district governor also had a personal militia that he used to protect himself and certain reconstruction projects. There were also militia fighters loyal to a local warlord and former governor of Kandahar Province, who kept the Taliban out of the southern part of Dand District. Canadian forces ensured that these different elements spoke to one another and coordinated their activities.

By the end of 2009, Deh-e-Bagh and the villages nearby were relatively stable and secure. Local contractors were running many projects independently, and attacks were few and far between. The company of Canadian soldiers and its team of engineers had achieved the short-term objective of stabilizing the area.

Near the end of 2009, community and district leaders from nearby Panjwayi District approached the company and its engineers and asked them to expand their employment program to the west. Panjwayi was a notoriously restive and violent area where Taliban influence was strong. The Canadians had found few leaders willing to cooperate with the Coalition until word spread of the endeavor in Dand.

The continued effort, however, remained heavily dependent on the presence of Canadian soldiers and engineers. The Canadians in Dand did not believe they had enough troops to expand their operations into the Panjwayi, despite the promising overtures by leaders there.

It was also unclear whether the gains made were sustainable, whether the effort could be transitioned from a military-led operation to a civilian one any time soon, or what effect stability in the small area in Dand District had on Kandahar Province as a whole. What is clear is that the experiment in Dand exceeded all expectations. The successes achieved there fundamentally altered perceptions of the Canadian presence in the surrounding area.

Conclusion

The oil-spot approach worked well in Dand District. As the progress made in Deh-e-Bagh became apparent elsewhere, it was easy for Canadian forces to expand into nearby villages, often at the express invitation of local leaders. The oil-spot approach was quite different than more ambitious clear-hold-build operations elsewhere, many of which involved clearing entire districts or groups of villages at once and setting up bases, with or without the consent of local leaders.

Canadian forces clearly adopted the right approach. That said, existing conditions in Dand District had a lot to do with the progress achieved there. Most of the people around Deh-e-Bagh were Barakzai tribesmen who tended to lean toward the government—as opposed to the Noorzai in neighboring Panjwayi to the west, who tended to side with the insurgents. Belanday Village, along the border with Panjwayi, was the most violent of all the villages in Dand. Panjwayi District was one of the most dangerous areas of Afghanistan, with a long history of armed resistance dating back to the war against the Soviets in the 1980s. The area around Deh-e-Bagh was placid by comparison.

Canadian soldiers and engineers focused their use of reconstruction funds on one objective: to employ as many fighting-age males as possible for as long as possible to
draw potential recruits away from the insurgency. With this in mind, the engineers focused on low-technology, labor-intensive projects that could be drawn out as long as possible. The objective was not to win hearts and minds—a vague and often unrealizable
goal—by providing public goods such as wells, roads, schools, and the like. The projects
themselves mattered less than the jobs they created.

This was particularly important in the villages around Deh-e-Bagh, where most local
people were sharecroppers. They did not own the land and so felt little ownership over
it. Infrastructure projects like wells, bridges, roads, canals, and the like improved yield
and increased the value of the land—but this mostly benefitted a handful of large land-
holders who did not always pass these gains on to the farmers who worked the fields.
Regular wages ensured the support of the majority of the population, especially those
unemployed fighting-age males most likely to join the insurgency.

The engineers' single-minded focus on job creation helped streamline the use of reconstruction funds. The engineers succeeded in tying much of the population to the
military effort. There was considerable evidence to suggest that the jobs the engineers
created lured many local recruits away from the Taliban and turned the population firmly
against the insurgents.

The soldiers dispersed into small outposts and patrolled on foot. They spent more time
outside their bases than any other unit in the province. They lived in the villages and interacted with locals every day. According to the company commander, "Living on the
FOB [forward operating base], you will not win. By living in small bases, you are always
talking to the people." Despite their vulnerability, these outposts were never attacked.
The company commander found that by dispersing his forces and doing regular patrols,
his troops were safer than they would have been in a handful of large, heavily fortified
bases. In neighboring Panjwayi District, where soldiers operated out of large bases and
conducted relatively few patrols, Canadian troops were under constant attack.

Relationship building was central, but doing it properly required great patience. According to the company commander, "You might go to five or six shuras and get
nothing. It might not be until the ninth shura that you get that little piece of useful

information." Officers spent hours chatting informally with local leaders and drinking tea—talking about their families, the harvest, the weather, anything to build rapport. The Canadians learned that this was how business was conducted in Afghanistan. According to the company commander, "Drinking tea and sitting in shuras is worth its weight in gold. You never talk shop right away. That's not the way it is done in Afghanistan. The first thing is always the social call."

Despite the successes they achieved, the engineers remained concerned about whether what they achieved could be sustained without a permanent military presence and an unending flow of cash. There were only so many Canadian soldiers and engineers to go around, and only so much money to spend. The more areas the soldiers expanded into, the more thinly spread they became. The more jobs they created, the more local people became dependent on outside funds.

The issue for the engineers was the need to hand their effort off to the Afghan government and civilian development agencies. They were also concerned that the tactical successes they achieved in the villages of Dand might not be adequately exploited at the strategic level. The same can be said of nearly every counterinsurgency operation conducted in Afghanistan to date.

Conclusion

The vignettes in this book contain many valuable insights about how relatively small units on the ground actually conducted counterinsurgency in Afghanistan. They shed light on the unique conditions these units faced, why they did the things they did, what yielded results, and what proved to be counterproductive.

The experiences of these units—in some of the most difficult and dangerous areas of the country—provide unique insights into the nature of the war in Afghanistan and highlight some of the challenges to come as U.S. and NATO forces draw down. For the most part, it will be up to locally based forces to implement a stable transfer of power district by district and firebase by firebase. Much of this will depend on the continued application of sound counterinsurgency principles adapted to local conditions.

As the United States draws down in Afghanistan, the critics of counterinsurgency and stability operations will no doubt insist that the military turn its attention back to conventional operations and not retain the lessons of Iraq and Afghanistan. This would be a mistake. While the United States must be prepared for major wars, the odds of actually fighting such wars are slim. It is mainly irregular conflicts where U.S. forces will be deployed for active combat operations. Future operations along these lines are likely to be much smaller in scale than recent conflicts, but the U.S. military must be prepared nonetheless.

Many of the themes touched on in this book will be of enduring relevance for future conflicts. The next places U.S. forces deploy in order to fight insurgents and restore order will likely be underdeveloped, war-torn countries like Afghanistan. No matter what happens in Afghanistan, U.S. forces will probably find themselves doing counterinsurgency and stability operations in other parts of the world in the not-too-distant future—be it in Libya, Yemen, the Horn of Africa, or even Pakistan. There will never be enough special forces for these tasks; conventional forces, especially the Marines, will be called upon to fulfill these missions.

The wars in Afghanistan and Iraq have created a battle-hardened force with unprecedented experience in dealing with civilian populations in situations of great flux and violence. This experience will be of great value to future forces, whether they are tasked with doing counterinsurgency, counterterrorism, peacekeeping, stability operations, or combat advising. This knowledge must be captured and retained, so that our ability to deal with complex internal conflicts may continue to improve.

Implications for the Drawdown in Afghanistan

The main focus of effort for the United States in the next few years will be on transitioning responsibility to the Afghan government and security forces, keeping these forces operational and united, preventing the Kabul government from collapsing, and sustaining the capability to strike against terrorist groups that threaten the United States. As before, it will be largely up to small units on the ground to ensure that these objectives are met—that districts remain stable as U.S. forces draw down, that army and police units in the field do not fall apart, and that intelligence on terrorist groups in remote border areas remains accurate and actionable.

Much of transition will unfold at the local level, with units in the field doing most of the work. Afghanistan's population is extremely fragmented, and likely to remain so. It is possible that the conflict in Afghanistan may have no national solution. If peace comes at all in the next few years, it will be due in large part to numerous small victories in the provinces and districts—the result of local political dynamics that military and civilian leaders in Kabul may never fully understand. If the drawdown unfolds smoothly in enough key districts, it may be possible to make up for some of the failures at the strategic level and with the government in Kabul.

In many districts in the south, especially in Helmand, U.S. and NATO forces have already negotiated agreements with the tribes and built viable governments. Strategic assessments and planning should be guided by local conditions and by the perspectives of units in the field who understand their areas better than anyone else. The larger-order challenge will be to make sense of local developments and capitalize on them at the strategic and policy levels. As units transition out, the local balance of power will change, causing political dynamics to shift. Understanding these changes and finding ways to manage them will prove an immense challenge.

It will be important to reassure local leaders and to draw down slowly while maintaining stability. Various leaders and power brokers are already posturing for an eventual U.S. withdrawal to ensure their interests and their survival. The Taliban could step up their assassination and intimidation of key Afghan leaders as American troops leave, or pull back and surge again when there are no longer enough foreign troops to fight back. If Coalition forces leave too quickly and a critical mass of progovernment leaders are killed or switch sides, it could create a snowball effect, leading to a resurgence of the Taliban and anti-American militant groups.

Hard decisions will have to be made about what areas are more and less important when it comes to larger political and strategic objectives. It will not be possible to keep forces everywhere there is violence. Unlike the cities of Iraq, Afghanistan's mainly rural population—spread out among thousands of small, often isolated villages—can only be partially controlled. There will be many areas in Afghanistan and Pakistan where insurgents will continue to find refuge. These areas may grow as the United States draws down. It will be imperative to keep the insurgency from overwhelming key areas and to keep it off balance long enough to allow the situation to stabilize.

As U.S. and NATO forces leave, it will ultimately be up to the Afghan army to keep the insurgency at bay and prevent a return to civil war. As of early 2011, few Afghan battalions were capable of operating independently; most will require embedded advisors for quite some time, in addition to air, logistics, medical, and other support. It will not be apparent how capable each Afghan unit is until it is given battlespace to control and faces serious pressure from the Taliban. The key will be whether the army can, with outside help, hold on to the capital and other crucial areas.

If history is any guide, the withdrawal of U.S. and NATO troops from Afghanistan could create a power vacuum for other regional players to exploit, each with their own particular interests and areas of influence inside Afghanistan. As the vignettes in this book show, Afghanistan remains an extremely divided society with a weak government. At every level there are factions engaged in bitter conflict looking for allies among rival outside forces. It may be necessary to step up pressure on Pakistan and insurgents operating in that country as the United States hands over security responsibility to Afghan units. Diplomats will have to engage with Afghanistan's other neighbors as well, especially Iran, India, Russia, and China.

In addition to funding the army, it would also be advisable to maintain the flow of funds to reconstruction projects and local defense forces. Units in the field have injected massive amounts of cash into local economies. These funds have created progovernment patronage networks that would soon crumble if the money disappeared. Many young men would be out of work and more inclined to join the Taliban. On the other hand, keeping funds flowing to reconstruction projects and local forces could serve as an important source of influence in the years to come.

Even if the United States withdraws most of its combat forces, it is likely that the counterterrorism mission will remain for some time. Though Osama bin Laden is dead, there remains a vast infrastructure of extremist militancy—of which al Qaeda is only a part—that straddles both sides of the border. As the vignettes in this book show, counterinsurgency and counterterrorism are closely linked. U.S. and Afghan forces will need to maintain the support networks they have painstakingly built over the years in the border areas if they are to keep tabs on terrorist groups and act against them.

Beyond Afghanistan

The lessons of Afghanistan will prove invaluable when U.S. forces again find themselves operating among civilians in another underdeveloped, war-torn society. It is often countries like Afghanistan—ungoverned, ruined by years of civil war and insurrection, with desperately poor populations scattered about in isolated rural communities—where extremist groups thrive and that foster the sort of chaos and violence that invites foreign intervention.

Countering a Rural Insurgency

Coalition forces in Afghanistan learned that operating among a highly dispersed population in rural areas poses unique challenges. Many small units operated out of extremely remote patrol bases, almost completely cut off from their higher headquarters. In this respect, conventional forces have been tasked with operating like special forces, who receive additional training and equipment in order to operate far from reinforcements. Soldiers and Marines learned how to adapt their approaches to the unique conditions in their areas. They developed accurate portraits of local politics, economics, and social norms, and came up with counterinsurgency tactics that fit these conditions.

Like rural insurgents everywhere, the Taliban moved easily across vast swathes of sparsely populated terrain. With limited forces operating among a widely dispersed population, it was extremely difficult to secure isolated villages. U.S. troops learned to accept that in such places, villagers and local officials are going to play both sides. It was not realistic to expect full cooperation from people whose security was not absolutely assured. Units also learned that raids and other combat operations are often ineffective and counterproductive in remote rural areas where it is difficult for outside forces to move undetected.

The most effective approach was to engage with villages as frequently as possible, use reconstruction funds to provide jobs and tie people into the government and the U.S. presence, and empower local leaders willing to resist the insurgency. The building of personal relationships based on trust was essential. This took time and patience. Local people in isolated parts of Afghanistan were inherently suspicious of outsiders and accustomed to governing themselves. Coalition troops realized that it was important to adopt a nonthreatening posture, so as to avoid inflaming the xenophobic tendencies of fiercely independent tribes. The more thoughtful officers and NCOs strived to understand the subtle differences between local resistance movements and true insurgent activity linked to the Taliban and other Pakistan-based groups.

In every local area, rival clans and power brokers struggled for influence, power, and access to resources. They fought constantly, often as a result of feuds that went back generations. The insurgents easily exploited these local rivalries. Soldiers and Marines learned that it was important to be careful about the alliances they formed with local power brokers, remain neutral in local disputes, treat the intelligence they received with skepticism, and be extremely circumspect when it came to targeting alleged insurgent leaders. Some units that failed to do so made enemies of entire clans and tribes, causing them to take up arms against the Coalition.

Some small units in remote outposts learned that they could rely on the population for their protection. Units tended to be quite safe in areas where people welcomed their presence, even if Taliban influence remained strong. Where the local people were hostile, security conditions for U.S. troops were very bad, even if they operated from large, well-fortified bases and had access to the best equipment and armored vehicles. Small units in particularly remote and dangerous areas lived under the constant threat of their bases being overrun and patrols being wiped out by large numbers of enemy fighters. For some troops in particularly dangerous and isolated places, building popular support was essential for survival—especially in villages near the base.

Units tasked with collecting intelligence for counterterrorism operations and targeting high-level enemy leaders learned to combine these activities with traditional counterinsurgency operations aimed at building a base of popular support. Special and conventional forces both learned that in remote rural areas, counterinsurgency and counterterrorism are closely linked. Despite stovepipes at the top, different agencies often worked quite well together at the local level. Units learned to coordinate with other civilian and military groups in their areas of operation and to work together in the absence of a unified command structure.

The Army and the Marines have learned to distribute their forces over vast areas and to operate out of small bases. This capability will prove useful in future situations where ground forces are sent to remote rural areas. When operating across huge expanses of sparsely populated terrain, units had to constantly grapple with the dilemma of how widely to spread their forces. Concentrating on small areas allowed troops to better protect a portion of the population and jump start reconstruction. But doing so left large areas under the control of the Taliban. Spreading out too far endangered outposts and lines of communication, and made it easier for the insurgents to infiltrate back into cleared areas. It was essential for officers at every level to consider the relative merits and dangers of concentration versus dispersion, and, when setting up certain patrol bases, to think about the potential implications months or years down the road. The dilemma was different in every place, depending on local politics, demographics, terrain, and other factors.

Working in a War-Torn Society

By 2001, Afghanistan had been in a state of civil war for 22 years. Constant fighting had deepened the divides between tribes and clans. Violence, rather than dialogue and negotiation, had become the primary means of settling disputes. Coalition troops that adopted a population-centric approach learned that one of the best means for building popular support was to help people resolve conflict peacefully. Units that were seen as honest brokers—aware of political fault lines but scrupulously neutral—achieved much with relatively little fighting.

Years of war had also split tribes into numerous factions and eliminated prominent tribal chiefs capable of enforcing unity. Many Coalition troops came to understand the importance of developing consensus through shuras and other consultative assemblies. They established security, enabling Afghan leaders to meet and negotiate without intimidation or fear of bloodshed, and brought marginalized groups into the political process.

In many places, a generation of internecine warfare had killed off or undermined much of the tribal leadership. Warlords and young men with guns held sway through fear. The traditional leaders were often there, but many did not have the power they once did. Units on the ground learned how to bring these traditional leaders back into politics—to identify them, protect them, and empower them. Marines and soldiers also learned how to engage constantly with the population despite daily attacks, to focus on the people and engage in peaceful negotiation even when under fire.

Like people in any war-torn society, Afghans were traumatized by a generation of indiscriminate violence—the worst of it inflicted by Soviet airpower during the 1980s. Villagers expected the United States to restore peace. Airstrikes and other combat operations that harmed civilian life and property caused many Afghans to think twice about supporting the U.S. presence. The heavy-handed, often belligerent, enemy-centered posture of many Coalition troops did not help either. Military officers who listened to the concerns of local people soon realized that it was essential to use restraint and discrimination in the use of force, even against local fighters known to be involved in attacks on U.S. troops. More violence was not the answer.

Spending Money in Underdeveloped, Agricultural Economies

Where people are so poor, a little money can go a long way—assuming it is spent wisely. A small well or micro-hydro project can transform a tiny village living on the edge of survival. A dirt road can open up isolated villages to commerce. Where there is little money or development, giving local officials or pro-government village leaders control over even small pots of money can empower these individuals considerably. In such places, reconstruction funds can be the most powerful tool in a unit's arsenal.

Yet outside money can also be destabilizing. It was important for officers to consider the unintended consequences of using reconstruction funds. For example, giving projects to one faction and not another often caused resentment and bred more violence. Funneling money through the wrong contractors or officials contributed to corruption. Heavy influxes of cash caused inflation that hurt poor farmers. The lure of inflated salaries drew people away from their farms, teachers away from schools, and doctors away from clinics—leading to negative consequences down the road when projects ended. In Afghanistan, the units that used their money most successfully were sensitive to these issues. They studied the local economy and considered the economic and political implications of each project.

Successful commanders thought carefully about what they wanted to achieve with the funds they had, and the best ways to employ that money toward those ends—keeping in mind the unique economic and political situation in their area. It was rarely a good idea to just throw money at the problem and scatter projects about, with the general aim of winning hearts and minds. Officers who used their money well thought carefully about the impact they wanted projects to have and how this related to other political and military objectives. In other words, they used their funds strategically as part of a coherent plan tailored to local conditions.

Building Local Governments from Scratch

When U.S. forces first arrived in Afghanistan, a generation of unrelenting violence had destroyed what little government the country once had. Small units on the ground had to build institutions almost from scratch. Coalition troops learned how to identify power brokers and traditional leaders and bring them into the political process. They also identified systems of unofficial village governance and came up with innovative ways to integrate them with district administrations. These units focused on connecting people to their government from the ground up. Strong and well-respected governors also helped. Successful units learned how to empower these governors and work through them.

U.S. and NATO forces learned to deal with local governments that were extremely corrupt and to advise and improve upon police forces that were often abusive, incompetent, full of drug addicts, and infiltrated by the Taliban. Units on the ground found ways to reduce corruption and professionalize the police, while providing space for the security forces to grow.

Marines and soldiers also managed to mobilize the population behind the counterinsurgency effort despite serious problems in the government. They did so by constantly engaging with the population, organizing regular shuras, and bringing local leaders into the political process. Most governments in underdeveloped societies have serious problems with disloyalty, corruption, and police abuse. The ability to overcome these obstacles will prove immensely useful in future interventions.

In late 2001, Afghanistan had no functioning army or police force. As the insurgency picked up steam, it became apparent that the United States and NATO needed to develop security forces capable of fighting insurgents and maintaining order with minimal outside support. National training programs turned out recruits in large numbers, but it was up to units on the ground to organize, train, and advise these forces. Small units also learned to raise and maintain irregular armed groups as a supplement to existing police and army forces.

Though raising and advising indigenous forces is a traditional special forces mission, much of this effort fell to conventional forces in the Army and Marine Corps. The more effective advisors lived with those they trained, patrolled and fought with them, and involved them in all aspects of planning—the ultimate goal being to get Afghan units to the point where they were willing and able to operate on their own with little or no Coalition support. The conflict in Afghanistan has produced a wealth of expertise in the U.S. Army and Marine Corps when it comes to raising and advising indigenous forces. It has also improved the military's understanding of just how central the training mission is in counterinsurgency and stability operations.

The Primacy of Politics

One of the most important lessons from the Afghanistan conflict is that counterinsurgency is not just about protecting the population and building up the government. It is about mobilizing the population, bringing in local leaders and forging political coalitions. That is how the Taliban and other insurgent groups operate. Everything they do is in pursuit of political objectives. Military operations and reconstruction projects are not always the best tool and may actually get in the way if not properly coordinated with political activities. It is vital for there to be clear political objectives, for forces to be deployed exclusively in pursuit of these goals, and for the strategy to be clear in the minds of units on the ground.

Counterinsurgency doctrine stresses protecting the population. Yet in several cases described in this book, the population protected U.S. and NATO forces, particularly in remote areas with a heavy insurgent presence. Where Marines and soldiers were able to build popular support, they were much safer; where they failed to do so, they came under constant attack, no matter how many forces or how much money was at their disposal.

In many cases, a smarter and less invasive approach, involving fewer personnel and less money, would have done more to weaken the insurgency and keep troops safe. In some cases, clear-hold-build was not the right approach at all. Reaching out to key leaders, negotiating, persuading them to support the government, and giving them what they need to do so from behind the scenes were often more effective methods than sending in large numbers of ground forces.

One of the main dangers of doing counterinsurgency, especially in underdeveloped countries like Afghanistan, is that the operation can become protracted and lead to mission creep. It is easy to get tied down and lose sight of the ultimate political objective and how to achieve it. The temptation to expand commitments, areas of operation, and the scope of activities (i.e., from chasing terrorists and guerrillas to providing security, building governments, developing the economy, and cracking down on drugs and corruption) is strong. Once forces are deployed in substantial numbers and new bases established, the United States becomes committed. One cannot abandon bases under fire without some appearance of defeat, which can have serious political and military consequences.

From the policy level all the way down to the tactical, it is vital for U.S. leaders to understand what they are getting into before deploying additional forces or sending them into new areas—to be circumspect about taking on new commitments without sufficient information, long-term planning, and a clear sense of the ultimate political objective.

Notes

Vignette 2: U.S. Marine Battalion, Nawa, Helmand, 2009

1. Mark Walker, "Local Marines Holding Ground in Helmand's Nawa District," *North County Times*, 25 July 2009.

2. Tony Perry, "Marine's Success in Afghanistan Has a History," *Los Angeles Times*, 31 December 2009, hereafter Perry, "Marine's Success in Afghanistan Has a History."

3. John McCall, "H&S Marines Guard the Perimeter of Patrol Base Jaker," *Leatherneck*, October 2009, 15–16.

4. Perry, "Marine's Success in Afghanistan has a History."

5. Michael T. Flynn, Matt Pottinger, and Paul D. Batchelor, *Fixing Intel: A Blueprint for Making Intelligence Relevant in Afghanistan* (Washington, DC: Center for a New American Security, 2010), 13. Online at http://www.cnas.org/node/3924.

6. Tony Perry, "Marines in Afghanistan Hear a Plea: Don't Leave Too Soon," *Los Angeles Times*, 23 November 2009.

7. Richard Tomkins, "Thanksgiving is a Hard Time for Marines," UPI, 25 November 2009.

Vignette 3: U.S. Marine Advisors, Tagab Valley, Kapisa, 2008

1. M. Hassan Kakar, *Afghanistan: The Soviet Invasion and the Afghan Response, 1979-1982* (Berkeley, CA: University of California Press, 1997), 286.

2. "Operation Al Hasn," *Infantry* (July–August 2007).

3. "Taliban Readies Ramadan offensive," Al Jazeera, 13 September 2007. Online at http://english.aljazeera.net/news/asia/2007/09/200852513105165396.html.

Vignette 4: U.S. Army Battalion, Kunar and Nuristan, 2007–2008

1. Gowardesh was the farthest advance the Soviet army had during the 1980s.

Vignette 5: U.S. Army Battalion, Khost, 2004–2008

1. Department of Defense (DoD), *Report on Progress Toward Security and Stability in Afghanistan*, Report to Congress, June 2008, 5, hereafter DoD, *Report on Progress Toward Security and Stability in Afghanistan*.

2. Brigadier Mohammad Yousaf and Major Mark Adkin, *The Bear Trap: Afghanistan's Untold Story* (Lahore, Pakistan: Jang Publishers, 1992), 159; Ahmed Rashid, *Taliban: Militant Islam, Oil and Fundamentalism in Central Asia* (New Haven: Yale University Press, 2000), 132.

3. For example, see Ann Marlowe, "A Counterinsurgency Grows in Khost: An Unheralded U.S. Success in Afghanistan," *The Weekly Standard*, 19 May 2008, hereafter Marlowe, "A Counterinsurgency Grows in Khost."

4. "CENTCOM Commander Attends Khost Leadership Conference," American Forces Press Service, 5 November 2007. Online at http://www.defense.gov/news/newsarticle.aspx?id=48048; Donna Miles, "Gates Lauds Progress in Afghanistan's Khost Province," American Forces Press Service, 4 December 2007. Online at http://www.defense.gov/news/newsarticle. aspx?id=48314.

5. Christopher Ives, *Interview with CDR John Wade*, Operational Leadership Experiences, (Fort Leavenworth, KS: Combat Studies Institute, 2008), 13, hereafter Ives, *Interview with CDR John Wade*.

6. Ibid.; Micah E. Clare, "Khowst PRT Winning the Fight in Afghanistan," *Army News*, 30 May 2007, hereafter Clare, "Khowst PRT Winning the Fight in Afghanistan." Online at www.army.mil/-news/2007/05/30/3404-khowst-prt-winning-the-fight-in-afghanistan/.

7. Ives, *Interview with CDR John Wade*, 13–14; former Khost PRT commander (March 2007–March 2008) comments at CNA roundtable on 13 May 2008.

8. In the fall of 2006, former Pakistani President Pervez Musharraf entered into a peace agreement with the Taliban fighting in Waziristan. See "Pakistan 'Taleban' in Peace Deal," BBC News, 5 Sept 2006. Online at http://news.bbc.co.uk/2/hi/5315564.stm.

9. Combined Joint Task Force-101, quoted in Tom Vanden Brook, "In Afghanistan, Path to Stability is Full of Challenges for Obama," *USA Today*, 12 January 2009.

10. The new campaign was known as "Protect the Quarterback." See "Policing a Whirlwind," *Economist*, 15 December 2007; Marlowe, "A Counterinsurgency Grows in Khost."

11. Ann Marlowe, "Anthropology Goes to War," *Weekly Standard*, 26 November 2007, 30.

12. Carter Malkasian and Gerald Meyerle, *Provincial Reconstruction Teams: How Do We Know They Work?* (Carlisle, PA: U.S. Army War College Strategic Studies Institute, 2009), hereafter Malkasian and Meyerle, *Provincial Reconstruction Teams: How Do We Know They Work?*

13. DoD, "DoD News Briefing with Cdr. Adams and Governor Jamal from the Pentagon," news transcript, 5 September 2007. Online at http://www.defense.gov/transcripts/transcript.aspx?transcriptid=4033; Marlowe, "A Counterinsurgency Grows in Khost," 22; Malkasian and Meyerle, *Provincial Reconstruction Teams: How Do We Know They Work?*

14. Malkasian and Meyerle, *Provincial Reconstruction Teams: How Do We Know They Work?*

15. DoD, *Report on Progress Toward Security and Stability in Afghanistan*, 11.

16. John J. Kruzel, "Commander Sees Progress in Afghanistan's Khost Province," American Forces Press Service, 5 September 2007; Ives, *Interview with CDR John Wade*, 17.

17. Tom Philpott, "Rebuilding a Nation: U.S. Navy Sailors Head a Half-Dozen PRT Teams Providing Hope for the Future in Afghanistan," *Seapower* (April 2007): 48 and 50; Ives, *Interview with CDR John Wade*, 2.

18. In 2006, Khost was one of the three provinces where UNAMA did not operate. See UNDP Afghanistan Annual Report, 2006:1. Online at http://www.undp.org.af/publications/index.htm.

19. Farah Stockman and Kamal Sadaat, "U.S. Alters Strategy, Makes Gains after Botched Raid," *Boston Globe*, 10 February 2008.

20. Robert J. Bebber, "Developing an IO Environmental Assessment in Khost Province: Information Operations at PRT Khost in 2008," *Small Wars Journal* (Febuary 2009), hereafter Bebber, "Developing an IO Environmental Assessment in Khost Province."

21. Ibid.

22. Casey Ware, "ANSF Assumes Control of Bak District Center," CJTF-101 press release, 22 August 2008.

23. Ann Marlowe, "In War Too, Personnel is Policy," *Wall Street Journal*, 14 June 2008.

24. Bebber, "Developing an IO Environmental Assessment in Khost Province."

25. Assassination attempts on Governor Jamal included suicide car bombs in August and October 2007 and a major attack on FOB Salerno in August 2008.

Vignette 6: U.S. Army Battalion, Nangarhar, 2005–2009

1. Nick Dowling and Tom Praster, eds., *Nangarhar Provincial Handbook* (Arlington, VA: IDS International, 2009), 3, 8, hereafter IDS International, *Nangarhar Provincial Handbook*.

2. The trade route known as Route 1 passes Jalalabad. Route 1 runs from Kabul through the Afghanistan border at Torkham Gate, the largest and busiest official border crossing to Pakistan.

3. Matthew Rosenberg, "U.S. Courts Former Warlords in Its Bid for Afghan Stability," *Wall Street Journal*, 20 March 2009, hereafter Rosenberg, "U.S. Courts Former Warlords in Its Bid for Afghan Stability."

4. Governor Sherzai did much less outside the city. See IDS International, *Nangarhar Provincial Handbook*, 29.

5. Sonia Winter, "Afghanistan: Radio Free Afghanistan Names 'Person of the Year,'" Radio Free Europe/Radio Liberty, 20 March 2008. Online at http://www.rferl.org/content/article/1079668.html; Matthew Rosenberg, "U.S. Courts Former Warlords in Its Bid for Afghan Stability."

6. David Mansfield, *Opium Poppy Cultivation in Nangarhar and Ghor* (Kabul, Afghanistan: Afghanistan Research and Evaluation Unit [AREU], 2006), 10, hereafter Mansfield, *Opium Poppy Cultivation in Nangarhar and Ghor*. Online at http://areu.org.af/EditionDetails.aspx?EditionId=198&ContentId=7&ParentId=7&Lang=en-US.

7. The U.S. military estimated that the Taliban collected $70 million annually, while the UN Office on Drugs and Crime estimated that the Taliban and its affiliates earned as much as $100 million each year from the drug trade. See Craig Whitlock, "Diverse Sources Fund Insurgency in Afghanistan," *Washington Post*, 27 September 2009. Online at www.washingtonpost.com/wp-dyn/content/article/2009/09/26/AR2009092602707.html.

8. United Nations Office on Drugs and Crime (UNODC), *Afghanistan Opium Survey 2004*, November 2004, 62. Online at http://www.unodc.org/unodc/en/crop-monitoring/.

9. Mansfield, *Opium Poppy Cultivation in Nangarhar and Ghor*, 9.

10. United Nations Office on Drugs and Crime (UNODC), *Afghanistan Opium Survey 2005*, November 2005, 29. Online at http://www.unodc.org/unodc/en/crop-monitoring/.

11. Farah Stockman, "Daughters Pay the Price in Poppy War," *New York Times*, 29 September 2005, hereafter Stockman, "Daughters Pay the Price in Poppy War."

12. United Nations Office on Drugs and Crime (UNODC), *Addiction, Crime and Insurgency: The Transnational Threat of Afghan Opium*, October 2009, 95. Online at http://www.unodc.org/unodc/en/data-and-analysis/addiction-crime-and-insurgency.html.

13. Stockman, "Daughters Pay the Price in Poppy War; Vanda Felbab-Brown, "Hasty Poppy Eradication in Afghanistan Can Sow More Problems," *Christian Science Monitor*, 23 March 2006; Sami Yousafzai and Ron Moreau, "The Opium Brides of Afghanistan," *Newsweek*, 7 April 2008, hereafter, Yousafzai and Moreau, "The Opium Brides of Afghanistan."

14. David Mansfield, *Pariah or Poverty? The Opium Ban in the Province of Nangarhar in the 2004/05 Growing Season and Its Impact on Rural Livelihood Strategies*, Project for Alternative Livelihoods in Eastern Afghanistan (PAL), June 2005, 12, hereafter Mansfield, *Pariah or Poverty?* Online at http://www.davidmansfield.org/all.php.

15. Mansfield, *Opium Poppy Cultivation in Nangarhar and Ghor*, 22.

16. The two tribes reportedly met prior to the planting season and agreed to plant poppy and resist eradication. See United Nations Office on Drugs and Crime (UNODC), Afghanistan Opium Survey 2007: Executive Summary, August 2007, 6–7. Online at http://www.unodc.org/unodc/en/crop-monitoring/; David Mansfield, *Resurgence and Reductions: Explanations for Changing Levels of Opium Poppy Cultivation in Nangarhar and Ghor in 2006-07*, Afghanistan Research and Evaluation Unit (AREU), May 2008, 15. Online at http://www.davidmansfield.org/field_work.php.

17. In 2007, governor-led eradication destroyed 2,339 hectares of opium poppy in Nangarhar Province. As a result, seven security incidents related to eradication occurred in the province that year. See United Nations Office on Drugs and Crime (UNODC), *Afghanistan Opium Survey 2007*, October 2007, 23. Online at http://www.unodc.org/unodc/en/crop-monitoring/.

18. David Mansfield, *'Poppy Free' Provinces: A Measure or a Target*, Afghanistan Research and Evaluation Unit (AREU), May 2009, 12, hereafter Mansfield, *'Poppy Free' Provinces*. Online at http://www.davidmansfield.org/all.php.

19. Gerry J. Gilmore, "Poppy-Free Nangarhar Province Shows Afghanistan Improvements," American Forces Press Service, 26 September 2008.

20. In April 2008, governor-led eradication eliminated only 26 hectares of opium poppy, compared to 2,339 hectares the year before. See United Nations Office on

Drugs and Crime (UNODC), Afghanistan Opium Survey 2008, November 2008, 72, 78. Online at http://www.unodc.org/unodc/en/crop-monitoring/.

21. The 750 soldiers in the task force spread out over four forward operating bases and two combat outposts. Mansfield, "'*Poppy Free' Provinces*," Afghanistan Research and Evaluation Unit (AREU), May 2009, 12.

22. United Nations Office on Drugs and Crime (UNODC), Afghanistan: Opium Winter Assessment, January 2009, 12.

23. Yousafzai and Moreau, "The Opium Brides of Afghanistan."

24. United States Government Accountability Office (GAO), *Afghanistan Drug Control: Strategy Evolving and Progress Reported, but Interim Performance Targets and Evaluation of Justice Reform Efforts Needed*, GAO-10-291, March 2010, 19.

25. DoD, "DoD Briefing with Lt Col Allison from the Pentagon Briefing Room, Arlington, VA, and Mr. Shawn Waddoups, Via Teleconference from Afghanistan," news transcript, 26 September 2008. Online at http://www.defense.gov/transcripts/transcript.aspx?transcriptid=4294.

26. David K. Spencer, "Afghanistan's Nangarhar, Inc: A Model for Interagency Success," *Military Review* (July-August 2009): 37. Online at http://usacac.army.mil/CAC2/MilitaryReview/repository/MilitaryReview_200908310001-MD.xml.

27. USAID Afghanistan, "Two Year Market Development Strategy Realizes Record Onion Sales, Contributes to Reduction of Illicit Crops," press release, 16 October 2008.

28. Jacob Caldwell, "Center Blazes Trail in Afghanistan Emergency Services," American Forces Press Service, 28 January 2008.

Vignette 10: UK-Led Task Force, Musa Qala, Helmand, 2006–2009

1. Anthony Loyd, "The Mysterious Warlord Trusted to Spread Peace in Divided Province," *The Times* (UK), 12 January 2008.

2. Mullah Salem was a veteran of the anti-Soviet resistance in the 1980s and was the Taliban governor of the southern province of Uruzgan prior to 2001.

3. Mullah Salem belonged to the Pirzai subtribe.

4. For example, on 30 August 2007, Taliban leadership council member Mullah Barader Akhund was killed in Sangin. See Ahmed Rashid, *Descent Into Chaos* (New York: Viking, 2008), 399. Also see "U.S. Steps Up Fight Near Major Taliban-Held Town," *New York Times*, 28 October 2007.

5. Stephen Grey, *Operation Snakebite* (London: Viking, 2009), 128, hereafter, Grey, *Operation Snakebite*.

6. An airstrike killed a Taliban senior commander, Mullah Ikhalas, on 2 December 2007. See "Several Militants Killed in Afghanistan Operation," American Forces Press Service, 5 December 2007.

7. Grey, *Operation Snakebite*, 7.

8. British troops included the 40 Commando Royal Marines Regiment, 2nd Battalion of the Yorkshire Regiment, and the 1st Battalion of the Scots Guards, supported by light tanks from the UK Household Cavalry Regiment.

9. Stephen Grey with the *Sunday* Times and Rupert Hamer with the *Sunday Mirror* were embedded with Royal Marines of the 2nd Battalion, Yorkshire Regiment.

10. "Two Taliban Commanders Killed in Afghanistan: U.S.," Agence France Presse (AFP), 16 December 2007; Fisnik Abrashi, "Troops Patrol Former Taliban Town," *USA Today*, 15 December 2007.

11. Anthony Loyd, "Former Drug Lord Koka is Nato's New Poster Boy and a Police Chief," *The Times* (UK), 11 July 2008.

12. The 2nd Battalion of the Royal Regiment of Scotland began training the ANP in Musa Qala. U.S. Marines briefly took over the responsibility of training the police and shifted it back to the British in early 2009.

13. House of Commons International Development Committee, *Reconstructing Afghanistan: Government Response to the Committee's Fourth Report of Session*

2007-08: Third Special Report of Session 2007-08, 24 April 2008, 7.

14. Under the direction of the Helmand provincial director.

15. Stephen Grey, *Operation Snakebite*, 304.

16. Institute for War and Peace Reporting, "Taleban Hamper Musa Qala Reconstruction Efforts,"ARR No. 311, 2 February 2009. Online at www.unhcr.org/refworld/docid/498beca18.html.

17. Governor Salem quoted in Ron Synovitz, "Afghanistan: Former Taliban Commander Advises U.S. Ambassador," Radio Free Europe/Radio Liberty, 16 January 2008.

18. Governor Salem quoted in Grey, *Operation Snakebite*, 319.

19. Local tribal elder quoted in Tom Coghlan, "Allies Prepare to Seize Taliban Stronghold," *Telegraph* (UK), 6 December 2007.

Vignette 12: British Army Advisors, Sangin, Helmand, 2009

1. Much of the population fled Sangin in 2006, only some of whom returned. "Cocktail of Ingredients Making Sangin So Lethal," BBC News, 8 March 2010.

2. Michael Yon, "Resurrection," *Michael Yon Online Magazine*, 2 August 2009. Online at http://www.michaelyon-online.com/resurrection.htm.

About the Authors

Jerry Meyerle is a political scientist in the Stability and Development Program at CNA. He is the author of several widely read studies on the insurgency in Afghanistan, as well as studies on the Afghan army and articles on regional security and political violence in Pakistan and India. Meyerle is a frequent speaker on these issues at conferences, seminars, and briefing sessions to deploying units and has also served on Afghanistan and Pakistan policy reviews for U.S. Central Command. In 2008, he was an advisor to the commander of the Kunar Provincial Reconstruction Team in eastern Afghanistan, where he worked on Pakistan border issues. He speaks Urdu and has a PhD in political science and South Asian studies from the University of Virginia.

Megan Katt is a research analyst in the Stability and Development Program at CNA. Most of her work at CNA has focused on various aspects of the insurgency and counterinsurgency in Afghanistan. Prior to joining CNA, she supported research on international security and national defense issues at the RAND Corporation. She holds an MA in international security studies from Georgetown University and a BS in business marketing from San Diego State University.

LtCol James A. Gavrilis, USA (Ret.), is a senior advisor in the Stability and Development Program at CNA. He is a former U.S. Army Special Forces officer with more than 24 years of experience in the infantry and special operations. Gavrilis has served overseas in Africa, the Balkans, and the Middle East in training, peacekeeping, and combat operations. He has commanded and directed operations focused on urban unconventional warfare, counterterrorism, and counterinsurgency. A graduate of the U.S. Army Command and General Staff College, he has an MA in international studies from Old Dominion University and a BA in political science from Pennsylvania State University.